TheSmartestWay™

TO

SAVE BIG

The Large Things in Life for Less

Samuel K. Freshman & Heidi E. Clingen

PRINTED IN THE UNITED STATES OF AMERICA

Copyright © 2016 Straightline Publishers, LLC

TheSmartestWay™ to Save Big, The Large Things in Life for Less

Library of Congress Control Number: 2015901541

ISBN: 978-0-9824746-6-2
[All Rights Reserved]

TheSmartestWay™ TO SAVE BIG

The Large Things in Life for Less

Samuel K. Freshman & Heidi E. Clingen

TheSmartestWay™ to Save Big
The Large Things in Life for Less

By Samuel K. Freshman and Heidi E. Clingen

FIRST EDITION
Straightline Publishers, LLC
"The Shortest Distance to Your Goal™*"*
Los Angeles, California, USA

Visit our website and sign up for free tips at
www.TheSmartestWay.com

Email us at
Heidi@TheSmartestWay.com

OUR MISSION

To help you spend less and save more, broaden your options, enrich your life with true value, and become financially independent.

DEDICATION

This book is dedicated to the readers of our first two books *TheSmartestWay™ to Save, Why You Can't Hang Onto Money and What To Do About It* and *TheSmartestWay™ Save More, Making the Most of Your Money.*

HOW TO READ THIS BOOK

Many readers tell us they decided to take "just a peek" at one chapter and ended up reading the rest of the book. On the other hand, you can briefly pick it up and find a solution that makes a difference in your life. It will inspire you to make easy and permanent changes that increase confidence in your ability to save. After you finish it and make your notes, pass it on. It is meant to be shared.

We want to acknowledge the artist Ros Webb for her illustrations of our cartoons.

Join our expanding community of savvy savers! Please share with us your personal savings story with us. Email a brief, approximately 500-word essay to Heidi@TheSmartestWay.com

TheSmartestWay™ to Save Big

The Large Things in Life for Less

INTRODUCTION

THIS IS OUR THIRD BOOK on how to save money. After we wrote *TheSmartestWay™ to Save, Why You Can't Hang on to Money and What to Do About It,* we wrote the second book in the series, *TheSmartestWay™ to Save More, Making the Most of Your Money.* We thought the first two books were the total of what we had to say on the topic. Were we ever wrong.

During the 2007 housing bubble, people delayed saving for retirement because they thought the inflated value of their home would stay afloat and borrowed on their home equity. When the bubble burst, more people were having trouble hanging onto their money. We decided to write book number two and now, number three to help you attain financial freedom.

Financial freedom means no worries about money. Lao-tzu wrote twenty-four centuries ago, "He who knows he has enough is rich." But how much is enough? That answer is different for everyone. It is knowing that you have saved and invested what you need to be comfortable in the lifestyle of your choice for the rest of your life—without having to work anymore.

Many have had let financial independence slip through their fingers. They invariably blow their chance on things they want but don't need. Lottery winners often drive their finances off a cliff after winning massive sums. The opportunity to become financially independent is presented to you throughout your life. How you handle both large and small purchases, is the difference between reaching and falling far short of your goal.

To attain financial freedom, learn to live below your income and be attentive to opportunities to save. Just as an example, getting your coffee free at your company's lunch room (rather than at a specialty coffee shop) can save anywhere from $1,000 - $1,500 in one year. Be smart about buying your home or your car and save thousands of dollars in one transaction. For example, 5-10% of the cost of acquiring a home (even a modest one, in the range of $150,000-$200,000) can result in savings of $10,000-$25,000.

Our earlier books are a great place to start your journey to financial independence. There, you can review Sam's *Principles of Financial Independence Part 1* in our first book and *Principles of Financial Independence Part 2* in the second book. If you apply them along with this book, it will be hard to make a mistake.

This book is about mindset. Mindset is how you think about something. You will have more money by saving more, which requires a positive money mindset. Saving money gives you options in life. As British business mogul Richard Branson says, "Money is for making things happen." Money is not the answer. What you do with it is the answer. Novelist and philosopher Ayn Rand wrote, "Money is only a tool. It will take you whereever you wish, but it will not replace you as the driver."

PART I:

Managing The Large Things In Life

Illustration by Ros Webb

"Sweetie, show me which keys you pushed when you changed
the pass code to Daddy's bank account."

Chapter 1

MANAGING YOUR MONEY MIND SET WITH THE BIG THINGS IN LIFE

EDUCATION

"An investment in knowledge always pays the best interest."
—Benjamin Franklin

MAKE THE MOST of your education dollars. Two-thirds of students borrow to pay for college. The average debt load is $27,000. For borrowers with graduate or professional degrees, the total debt ranges from $30,000 to $120,000. Some graduate with more than $200,000 in debt.

College gets more expensive every year. Nationwide, the average price of a college education has increased by nearly 130% in the past 20 years, according to the nonprofit College Board. Nevertheless, as Henry Ford said, "The only real security that a man will have in this world is a reserve of knowledge, experience, and ability."

Is college the right path?

Consider non-college professions. Technical schools or working as an apprentice for a business. Community colleges have two year trade program degrees. Consider training for being a plumber, electrician, ultrasound technician, a construction manager, radiation therapist, court reporters, paralegals, medical billing administrators, emergency medical technicians, and air traffic controllers. These jobs may pay well due to overtime or union support. Many commissioned sales jobs do not require a college education.

Don't let anyone tell you that trade school is not a viable option. Those trained in trades that are in constant or high demand can earn as much or more than white-collar professionals. Or you can start out in an entry level position of a field to find out if you like it, such as become a paralegal before you go to law school, become a medical or dental assistant before you go to medical or dental school. Heidi's dentist mentored one of his young assistants to get into dental school. The assistant has the enthusiasm and drive to complete his training because he knows first-hand that he loves his field. The medical field will be booming in the decades to come, due to the aging population.

Encourage your child to explore all options. Can he or she take a technical class to see if there is compatibility of interest and skills? Can he or she take some college courses while going to high school, to get a head start and experience in a selected field? Select colleges that specialize in that field. Take a hard look at average salaries in those fields. To get the latest figures, check out www.Payscale.com. Expend your resources based on the salary that the degree will offer. For example, someone who wants to be a preschool teacher should take out fewer loans than someone who wants to be an engineer. Today with high unemployment, many overqualified workers are competing for fewer jobs. A big payoff from a college education is not what it used to be.

In some areas of the country, there is a mad scramble to get children into an Ivy League school. There is the prestige for the family and social pressure. However, your children may receive a full scholarship at a school that offers their desired major, even if it is not a prestige school. Encourage your child to select a career first and then a school.

Take a look at the motivation to go to college

We believe in higher education, college or advanced trade school. Higher education is an excellent business plan for your life. These days, a bachelor's degree, which Heidi has, is the entry-level minimum for many jobs. Sam has a law degree which has served him well, even though he retired from his law practice and went into real estate development many years ago.

Explore your childrens' motivation to go to college and see if there are some cost-saving and time-saving alternatives. Do they just want to get away from home? If that's all they want, help them get an apartment nearby or in another state for a few months, until they sort out what they want to do with their lives. As we have said, there are multiple paths to success in life. Before the college path is selected as a default, make sure that your child is academically inclined and motivated? "Everyone else is doing it" is not enough of a reason to spend precious years and funds after high school.

It has been said that a college degree adds to your lifelong bank account. That has merit sometimes, but it depends on what degree. If you are considering an advanced degree, take a look at how much more money that degree should help you earn. When Sam graduated from law school, it was a safe bet that you could get a job after graduating. But times have changed. Consider that the average public law school student graduates with more than $70,000 in debt and the average private law school student graduates with more than $90,000 in debt. Also, the number of unemployed law school graduates is increasing. There are more graduates and fewer jobs. Big firms have cut back their associate programs. Lawyers who do have jobs are making less.

Think seriously before you sign the dotted line for a huge student loan. Is the degree you're earning going to earn you enough money to pay back your loan? An education is an investment, like buying property. You want a high probability that it will pay you back generously in the near future. You can take a year or two off to work, save money, and gain "real world" experience in your field. This could help you stay solvent. Sometimes an advanced degree may be less valuable than a degree in the school of hard knocks. Some who have earned Ph.D. degrees are disappointed to find that they end up being low-paid researchers. Little more than half of those students who start doctoral programs finish their degree.

A clear-headed perspective and balancing priorities is required these days. Perhaps you could be paying a real mortgage and supporting a roof over your head instead of mortgaging your future to a well-intentioned institution of higher learning.

Parents and saving for college

Parents are a partner in their child's decision to get further education, especially if they are paying for it. Many teens planning to attend college don't carefully consider all the issues and costs associated with attending the college of their choice. Parents should start talking about post-high school plans when the children are in middle school or junior high. Let them know that their grades and extra-curricular activities will all be important. In their junior year they will begin studying for the PSAT, which will help them qualify for a National Merit Scholarship.

Take a close look at your child. If he or she doesn't seem focused enough to select and graduate from a profitable, reasonably priced college program, have some serious discussions. You don't want huge college loans to ruin your child's financial stability or your retirement years.

When parents pay for college, studies show that an alarming 23 percent of the funds they provide come from their retirement savings. This can be risky because of tax penalties and other fees to withdraw money from retirement plans. Remember, you can borrow for college, but you cannot borrow for retirement. Some Baby Boomer parents give everything up for their children. Single mothers have to be especially careful to not make a long-term financial mistake, since they do not have a partner to help them save for retirement.

If you want to save for your children's college expenses, consider 529 plans. 529 Plans are contributions that go into pre-selected mutual funds. They grow tax-free each year. Withdrawals to pay tuition are tax free. However, there is no assurance your child will go to college. Also, the money you put into the plans may be better invested elsewhere. So ask a lot of questions about your college savings strategy before you decide.

When you pay for your children's education, require that they get a job to help. Post high school, your child could work a year or two before going further in their education or work part-time while they are studying. They will appreciate their education much more.

Sam took that idea one step further while in college and law school. His parents offered to mail him funds to cover his expenses. He put their checks in the bank and paid for everything himself by running the dormitory laundry, selling ads and managing the advertising department of the campus newspaper, as well as running a boarding house. When he graduated, he was debt free and had a sizeable nest egg with which to start his professional life. He says his campus jobs experience taught him far more about operating a business than his classroom studies. Also, students' experience at entry-level jobs in the work world will help motivate them to attain their degree in order to qualify for better positions.

College shopping is a major project

Help your child compile a list of at least 10 schools of interest. Make sure that they offer the major that your child is interested in. While college shopping, warn your child about falling in love too fast with a campus. A choice of college may be the first adult decision they make. Teens are less equipped than their parents to make a rational judgment about the consequences of a college choice. There are many factors to consider, such as does this institution meet their educational goals and is it affordable. Some parents even offer their children a cash bonus in exchange for choosing a more affordable college. Sometimes parents dream of their children attending "legacy" schools but this dream needs to be balanced with the realities of cost-benefit analysis of the true value of the degree.

When making the choice for which college to attend, peer pressure from family or friends can be hard to deal with. In some circles, an elite college degree is the gold standard that validates both the parents and the students in society. However, in the final analysis, unless family or friends are going to offer to help pay off the college debt, the decision belongs to the child and parent.

You can take one- to two-hour walking tour videos of hundreds of schools at www.CampusTours.com and www.eCampusTours.com. There are two day virtual college fairs at www.CollegeWeekLive.com. At the virtual fair, you can talk with admissions counselors and students via webcam.

If you visit in person, which is always a good idea, try to combine the trip with a holiday weekend, schedule two visits in one day, share expenses with another student and eat at the campus dining hall to get a flavor of the campus. Talk to students randomly. Also, get the school alumni newsletter and contact alumni. If you want to visit a large number of colleges in your region, you can hire a college tour company such as www.CollegeExlorations.com, and www.EducationUnlimited.com, for a wide array of college tours.

While shopping for college, bring a pencil

Help your child decide on the best education for the best price. Many elite schools cost more than $50,000 per year, compared to a third of the price for state universities. Community colleges and online schools are also an option.

It is easy at any college to underestimate the costs of housing, food, books, transportation, and the many "incidental" expenses such as clothes and entertainment. Then there is the temptation to study abroad for a semester, which can be expensive. Some college cost calculators assume that a four year degree will be achieved in four years. That is becoming less routine. With each year the student is in college, the expenses rise.

Make sure that the calculations pencil out. Finances are one of the most important factors in the decision about which school to attend. The most important factor is whether this school will meet your child's career needs. Several websites compare colleges, such as usnews.com/best-colleges, Princeton-Review.com/college-rankings, and www.TheDailyBeast.com. Students rate the colleges at www.StudentsReview.com. The National Center for Education Statistics' College Navigator site lets you compare the tuition and fees and financial aid at your targeted schools at www.nces.ed.gov.

When comparing financial aid packages, compare apples to apples, so to speak. Some costly private schools are so generous with their aid that they may be less expensive than a public school in the final analysis. Also, not all financial aid is made alike, so try to do a side-by-side chart that shows all the factors of each school and their cost and aid packages.

Subtract the value of the scholarships and grants from the (full) cost of attendance at each school. If you need help estimating the full cost of attendance, go to www.CollegeBoard.com or www.CollegeNavigator.gov. As a guide, don't borrow more for a degree than you expect to make the first year out of college. Check out the U.S. Department of Labor Statistics, which tracks pay for various occupations.

Take a look at scholarships and grants

Scholarships and grants don't have to be paid back. Therefore, they are your first goal. If your student is inclined toward physical and academic rigor, ways that the government can help him or her get a college education: ROTC scholarships can cover tuitions costs even at some elite private institutions. Use the scholarship search service on the College Board website.

If your student doesn't have a perfect GPA or doesn't fit a certain profile, make plenty of time to research scholarships and grants anyway. You may believe that your family income is too high to qualify, but some families with incomes of more than $100,000 may qualify. This is one of those areas of life where "You never know until you try" applies.

When you apply, do not be modest. Create a brag list of all of your accomplishments. Share that list with your school counselor and everyone else who can help you get funds for college. Find lesser-known local scholarships. Look on your school's and other schools' websites. Watch for newspaper articles about students who win scholarships and apply for scholarships yourself. Search online for scholarships on www. fastweb.com and www.finaid.org. When you find scholarships and loan opportunities, apply for them as soon as possible— before you even know if you want to go to that school.

Companies, trade groups, chambers of commerce, and non-profit organizations offer thousands of dollars in scholarships each year. It is your job to find them. When aid is offered, carefully analyze it with competing aid letters to see how they compare—for each school. Add up the value of scholarships and grants offered and list it under the cost figure. Work-study programs provide jobs on campus or in the community with hours tailored around a student's schedule and area of study.

Take a look at loans

Loans are easier to get than they are to pay off. Private student loans can require a cosigner. Private loans are more costly and offer few relief options. Federal student loans do not require cosigners, so students can get into trouble without parents' supervision. Federal loans offer options such as forbearance, extended terms and alternative repayment. You may be able to temporarily stop making payments on federal loans, although interest will continue to pile up

In most cases, interest on student loans begins accumulating from the day the loan is taken out. That means if you borrow $10,000 at a 5 percent interest rate, you will owe $10,500 at the end of one year and $11,025 at the end of the two years. So don't waste any time getting to graduation day. Have career track and a target graduation day clearly in mind before you sign for a loan. You need to have something to show for your expensive investment in the end. One of the worst things you could do is bury yourself in debt and leave college without a degree.

Don't become like the many graduates today who are heavily burdened by their loans, forcing them to put off buying a home, getting married, or having children. Don't let indebtedness reach the point where you have to pay $1,000 per month for ten or fifteen years. Shop around for good loans. Try finding a non-profit agency that specialized in education loans. The Consumer Financial Protection Bureau, a federal agency that helps make borrowing costs clear has a lot of tips. Check out www.apps.usa.gov/studentaid-gov.shtml.

If you are entering a Ph.D. program, you should not pay anything out of pocket. There are many fellowships, grants, and assistantships available. There are various types of loans, such as Stafford loans, subsidized Stafford loans, federal student loans, and Pell Grants. To learn your options, consult an expert college counselor.

Do the FAFSA

If you decide you are going to need to take out some loans, the FAFSA is in your future. The Free Application for Federal Student Aid, or FAFSA is vital to getting financial aid for college. Loans are offered based on need as determined by the FAFSA and the schools' financial aid office. The application determines the expected family contribution or EFC. This amount is subtracted from the cost of a college to determine the student's need for aid. The form includes more than 100 questions and work sheets, some of which can be complex, www.Fafsa.ed.gov. The form is free. Download the application and information early so that you can gather the necessary information for you and your child in time. You have to fill it out only once per year, no matter how many colleges you apply to.

Avoid careless and potentially fatal application errors. Read the directions three times and follow them closely. Note that you do not include the equity in your home and the money in qualified retirement accounts such as IRAs and 401(k)s. The biggest mistake that parents make is including exempted assets. If you include them, it will cost you thousands of dollars in aid.

The secret to FASFA success is timing. Submit the forms far in advance of deadlines. You don't need to complete your tax returns before you fill it out. If you wait until your taxes are done, you are likely to miss out. College counselors recommend you answer questions about income by estimating. You can revise your form later.

Assistance is usually based on the student and parents financial conditions from the previous year. Start planning early. Pay off credit cards with cash before filling out the aid form. This will help you qualify for more aid. If you need help, contact the school's financial aid office as soon as possible. Ask for financial aid as soon as you realize you need it, even if you are in the middle of a college term.

If your student takes a year off to get some work experience, plan ahead. Under financial aid formulas, student income is supposed to be routed to college. The money that was made during the year working will reduce the financial aid offered. Be sure to put their savings in the appropriate place. If you put it into the wrong place, it could hurt their chance of getting financial aid. Students are expected to contribute a higher percentage of their savings to their college education than their parents because they usually are not supporting a family. Most of the money placed in accounts in your student's name will be required in the financial aid calculations.

Save on expenses

Think twice before you pull out your wallet for anything. For example, you may not need a car. Keeping a car on campus requires a parking permit and parking tickets for parking in the wrong space can add up. Your auto insurance premiums may drop if you have your college student leave the car at home. You can borrow a friend's car or rent one when needed. They can use a bike, the bus, or carpool.

They should use the campus health center for routine visits and procedures. Also, there may be a campus counseling center, which is less expensive than regular therapy sessions, if the stress of college and adult issues start to get in the way of happiness and productivity. They may feel pressure to join a sorority or fraternity, but remember that they can be expensive. College students can save money with www. groupon.com and www.livingsocial.com and by participating in the many free cultural, social, and entertainment activities on campus. Recycle and never buy new. For clothes, try www. buffaloexchange.com and www.pawngo.com, and for furniture, try swap meets, thrift shops, and yard sales. Save now and enjoy later, after you graduate. Not the other way around.

A huge problem for students is credit card debt. Students are more focused on their GPAs than their FICOs, but their FICO score is a score that helps them succeed the rest of their lives. Students will need to watch every penny while in college. They should be on a cash basis with specific amounts in designated envelopes. It is easy to become buried in credit card debt. Students need education on how and when to use credit cards and how to pay their bills in full and on time every month. If they can handle a credit card, they need to find one with no annual fee and a low interest rate, check out www.creditcards.com and www.bankrate.com, and www.IndexCreditcards.com.

Save on textbooks

You can save money on college textbooks with a bit of planning ahead. Be ready to get the first available used books by getting the required book list as soon as possible and start shopping immediately. Remember, you are competing with all the other students in the class to get the best deal. Go to the campus bookstore, write down the ISN numbers. Be sure you are buying the right edition of the book. Returns and exchanges take valuable time that could set you behind in class. At the bookstore, note the prices for both new and used versions. Then shop online at www.amazon.com, www.BarnesandNoble.com, www.VarsityBooks.com, www.efollet.com, www.chegg.com, and www.ichapters.com. Use the comparison shopping site www.BestBookBuys.com.

You can download many classics of literature and other books at www.Gutenberg.org. Also check out the school library for their free copies. If you make friends who are studying for the same degree, try to share and swap books with them. When it is time to sell your books back, find out what the campus bookstore will pay you. Then compare with www.eBay.com, www.amazon.com and www.eCampus.com.

Find extra funds to pay for loans

Ask your employer to help you by including debt repayment in your compensation package. Your boss may be inclined to offer lower wages in exchange for a onetime payout for your loan because it costs them less in salary payments in the long run. Bring it up during salary negotiations or annual review. They may be motivated because they save. You will save money over time because you will eliminate the debt, raise your credit score, and pay much less interest.

Keep a lid on spending, create a budget, and figure out how to earn more money. This will help your credit rating, too. If you find that you need to return home after attending college, there needs to be a family meeting. As a "boomerang kid" you will need to help with chores and paying household expenses, and you will need to follow your parents' "house rules" if you want your home to be a harmonious place. Your parents may be able to write off some of your college bills with the American Opportunity Tax Credit.

Young people today will live longer and thus their retirement funds need to be larger than their parents. Unfortunately, lower employment and fewer job benefits await them, in addition to rising prices for housing, health insurance, gas, and basic necessities. To get a strong financial start in life, they need to stay out of huge college debt or to get rid of it as soon as possible.

CARS

"One man pretends to be rich, yet has nothing; another pretends to be poor, yet has great wealth."
—Proverbs 13:7-8

SOME PEOPLE spend more on their car, between insurance, taxes, license fees, repairs, maintenance and financing, than they do on their residence. As the joke goes, "Car sickness is the feeling you get when the monthly payment is due."

All of the costs of a car, including amortization of a loan, are an expense. Also remember that most cars do not increase in value over time. A home and its utility do not disappear. Over time, it may increase in value. You will still have the house when it's paid off and while it is increasing in value. But a car ordinarily has diminished to nominal value by the time the loan to acquire it is repaid.

Be smart about which car to choose

Decide what you need, not what you want. Do you really need a sport sedan? How many kids do you usually have in your car? Do you really need a luxury truck? How many loads of lumber do you haul every month? Make a list of your top three must-haves. Do you drive a lot and need excellent mpg? Do you have a large family and must have a lot of seating?

Remember that gas mileage really counts. For example the difference between a car that gets 20 mpg and one that gets 40 mpg ads up to $3,000 over five years. If you choose a car that uses 25 miles per gallon over 15 miles per gallon, you could save over 2,000 gallons of gas over 80,000 miles. At $3 a gallon, that's $6,400 in savings. Go to www.fueleconomy.gov to find out the fuel efficiency ratings for cars built since 1985. You will pay more for a popular car because the dealer is less willing to negotiate a deal. Also, choose a model that has a good safety record and a low theft rate.

After you make your top-three must haves list, ask your mechanic for his recommendation. Then pick three or four cars that you like and then comparison shop. Test drive several vehicles. Practice going in and not buying. It's an excellent exercise. You can find out which dealers you like and which dealers like you. If you don't like the answers or you don't like how you are being treated, go to another dealership. Not all dealerships are made alike, but they are all competing with each other for your business. Eventually you will find two dealers that are okay and when you are ready to buy, you will play them off each other.

Be smart about shopping for a car

As we said in our first book, whenever possible buy a used car and buy it for cash. You will never go wrong. If you must finance a car, take the shortest available loan length so you will pay less interest.

Your car is always depreciating, which is why taking out a car loan is usually a bad business deal. Before the loan is paid off, you may owe more than the car is worth. To make matters worse, if you buy the car at the end of the lease, it may cost you more in total than purchasing it at the outset.

After you decide if you are buying or leasing, window shop online at www.Consumer Reports.com and www.SaferCar. gov for reliable safety test results, at Automotive Lease Guide, www.alg.com, which shows depreciation value ratings, and www.Edmunds.com for a lease calculator and "true cost to own" information. At www.CarPrices.com you can find out the Manufacturer's Suggested Retail price (MSRP, often called the "list price") and the dealer's invoice price, which is the wholesale price that the dealer paid. The MSRP does not include any additional options. Go to www.TrueCar.com to find the lowest price: input in your location and the model you are looking for and it generates a graph charting the price of recently closed sales. For a monthly newsletter detailing available manufacturer-to-dealer incentives, check out www. Carbargains.org.

Be smart about buying a used car

If you can't afford to pay for a car in full and you don't qualify for a car loan, you may be tempted to shop at a "we sell to anyone" dealer. Be very careful. Make sure you buy a good, safe car you can afford, and that you calculate the interest rate you will be required to pay.

Legally, the dealer must give you a "buyer's guide". Beware of used car dealerships that are brand new, change names often or move around a lot. To make sure that the dealership is legitimate, check with the Department of Motor Vehicles, the Motor Vehicle Dealer Board and your local Better Business Bureau.

When you find a good used car, look it over carefully for what looks like a new paint job over damage. When you test drive it, make sure that the dashboard air-bag indicator lights up momentarily when the car is started and then goes off. If it stays on or blinks, there could be a problem with the air bag system. Then go online with the VIN number to get a vehicle history from www.CarFax.com, www.AutoCheck.com and www.nmvtis.gov. There you will find out the car's history. Ask the seller directly if the car has been in an accident. Before you buy it, have an independent mechanic that you trust check it out for mechanical, frame and electronic problems.

Look before you leap, as they say. If you change your mind after you sign the contract, the dealership is not obligated to take it back, unless they offer refunds in the contract. In many states used and new car buyers have a right of rescission for a short period. Find out about this before you buy. Do not drive the car off the lot until financing is final. You can get information and buy a full report on the car you are considering at www.CarFax.com and Kelly Blue Book, www.kbb.com.

Know how to decide between buying and leasing

The main difference between buying and leasing is that with a purchase, at the end of the payment period, you own the car. At the end of paying for the car lease, you hand the keys back to the dealer and walk away. The next biggest difference between buying and leasing is that with leasing your monthly payments are usually lower than a car that you are purchasing with financing.

When you buy a car, you can put as much mileage and wear and tear on the car, but this will lower its trade-in or resale value. If you decide that you don't want the car anymore or have to get rid of it, if you are financing the purchase, you will have to pay any pay-off amount and with a lease you would pay early termination charges.

With buying, your upfront costs may include the cash price or a down payment, taxes, registration and other fees. With leasing your up-front costs may include the first month's payment, a refundable security deposit usually equal to the first month's payment, a capitalized cost reduction, taxes, registration, and other fees.

If you don't pay for the car in cash, you need to make your payments. If you have to take out a loan for your car, do so wisely. As Earl Wilson said, "If you think nobody cares if you're alive, try missing a couple of car payments." When you shop around for a car, the inquiries from dealers counts as only one inquiry, as long as you do it within a few weeks. Multiple inquiries can ding your credit score. Ask up front if the car dealer plans to check your credit record when you buy a car.

Check out www.Autofinancing101.org/learningsuite for financing calculators and www.Bankrate.com or www.eloan. com for more information about financing a car.

If you drive a lot and wear out your cars, a lease will be even more expensive for you. Leases aren't for people who drive more than 10,000-20,000 miles per year, because beyond that mileage, you pay a penalty. Be realistic about how many miles you plan to drive over the lease period.

Be smart about negotiating

When car shopping, arrive prepared with your research. Focus on the invoice price, what the dealer paid, not on the MRSP or list price. Ask specifically, "Is this the price for the car I want with the equipment I want?" The sales associate will say it is way too low, but will take your offer to his sales manager and see what he can do for you. Don't just sit and wait, wander around looking at other cars.

Shop at the end of the year when the dealer is ready to make a deal to get rid of the old models and make room for the new models. Whatever you do, don't walk into the first dealership you can find and announce, "I am going to buy a car here, and I'm going to buy it today." The sales associate's eyes will light up because they know they will have an easy sale.

Never say that you love the car, you need it right away, or that you have bad credit. If you have a trade in, don't tell them until you have negotiated the purchase price of the car you are buying. Don't bring it with you when you are shopping. They will want to take a look at it, you will give them the keys, and that will put you in a weaker position with negotiations.

These are classic negotiators tips that work at the dealership: don't be in a hurry, never say yes to the first offer, listen carefully, ask a lot of questions, and ask for lots of extras. When they make their first offer, don't respond right away. Ask if they can do better. When they have come down as far as they say they can come down be quiet, then say "I'm sorry, you'll have to do better than that." Leave if you are still not satisfied, they may call you back with a better offer. Is good to bring a friend who knows about cars with you.

Be smart about add-ons

When shopping for a car, sales associates can give you data that will help you make an educated decision about which model to consider. Then they start trying to pile on the accessories and additional features to your bill. The showroom model is "loaded" with all the features, so customers can see what they look like and try them out. Sales associates are trained to try to dazzle you with the showroom model. You know that is the one they want to sell you to move that car off the lot. Tell them that you don't want the extras. Don't let them tell you, "The add-ons don't cost that much." In fact, the dealer often makes 15% on the base price of the car and 40% on the extras. Ask them to search for a model without the extras. Their auto exchange systems can find exactly what you want if you are willing to wait for it.

Here is Sam's approach: Start with the expensive item, and then the "little" items seem less expensive. In other words, say, "Great, you'll throw (large item) into the deal. Now, how about (little item)?" If they have said yes to the big, it is a little harder to say no to the little. Or if they said no to the large, when you ask for the little items, as kind of a consolation prize, it is harder for them to say no. It looks too selfish on their part. On the other hand, if you ask for the small first and they say yes, and then you ask for the large, it looks too greedy on your part. Ask for the big, then the small. It's a timing thing.

They will offer you an extended warranty, which may make sense if you are sure you will keep your car for five years or more. Ask what it costs, when it kicks in and what it covers. So called "power train only" warranties may exclude expensive electronic repairs common in today's cars. As we said in our first book, many experts believe that long-term warranties are not worth the cost.

It's all about timing. Making them wait for the sale gives you bargaining power, because they will be wondering if you are comparison shopping while you are waiting. The more work they put in to make the sale with you, the more willing they will be to cave in to your demands as you continue to play hardball. If there is an extra you want, negotiate to get it thrown in for free.

Know how to lease

If you are forced to lease a car, here are some tips to minimize the financial pain: Take the shortest lease length you can afford, to save on the interest. If you have bad credit, the rate will be higher. Wait until you raise your credit score and then you may qualify for get a lower interest rate, which could save you thousands of dollars over time.

First find out the cost and interest rate. You want them both to be as low as possible. Then look at the cash back incentive, the size of the down payment, the length of the lease and the miles allowed.

Find out what is the residual value of the vehicle—an estimate of what the car will be worth at the end of the term. This is the car's resale value when you are done with the lease. The value will be less because of depreciation, or lost value. The dealer will give you that amount as what you can pay to purchase the car at the end of the contract. Purchase-option fee is the fee you would pay in addition to the purchase price if you purchased it at the end of the lease. All this varies depending on the lender funding the transaction. Make sure that any lease includes gap insurance, which covers any gap between the amount the insurance company will pay if the car is ever totaled in an accident and the value the lease company has assigned to the car. Make sure the warranty period matches the lease period. Never lease a car longer than the warranty. You also want a closed-end lease, which means that you can walk away from the lease with no further expenses, as long as there is no unusual or "excess" wear and tear and no excess miles. Ask if there will be early termination fees, which are a penalty to end the lease before the term is discussed.

To get a better deal, learn "lease lingo." These are terms that can make the whole car leasing process less confusing. Here are some terms you should know: APR: This is the annual percentage rate, including the interest rate and other charges. If it is fixed, it will not change, if it is variable, it will usually increase over time. Allowable mileage: How many miles you can drive before you start to incur a penalty. Capitalized cost: also called the payoff amount, which is essentially the selling price, which you want to get down as low as possible. The drive-off fees are the cash you have to pay to take possession. The money factor is the interest rate. You multiply it by 2,400 to get the interest rate. Monthly payment: what you pay monthly for the lease or finance. Be sure to make sure taxes are included in this figure. Security deposit: the amount that you pay upfront.

Be smart about repairs

A well-maintained newer car should run for 150,000 miles or more before needing major repairs. Maintenance is important and worth the money to proactively keep your car in good shape. Use the maintenance schedule on your manual, despite what the dealer or the repairman may tell you. Keep a logbook in your glove compartment of every repair done to your car, which repair shop performed the work, and when. Independent repair shops will be less expensive than the dealer's shop. But make sure that it is ASE certified by the National Institute for Automotive Service Excellence. You can see a list of AAA Approved Auto Repair shops at www.aaa.com/repair.

Overzealous repairmen should be avoided. They recommend unnecessary repairs and treatments such as "de-carbonization," fluid "flushes," and filling your tires with nitrogen. You will read differing advice about how often to change your oil. Read your owner's manual and stick with that number of miles.

You can save up to 50 percent on tires by buying Goodyear's second-tier brand, Republic and Fierce. Don't buy tires over four years old. If you keep a record about your car, you will know when you last bought tires. Buy a tire gauge and make sure to keep them properly inflated and make sure that they have enough tread and that the tread wear is even. Rotate the tires regularly.

If an errant rock dings your windshield, have the crack filled right away by a windshield repair specialist. Otherwise, the crack will spread and you will have to replace the entire windshield. Take the car into the repair shop if you see the check engine light, or if you hear squeaks or grinding noises or see colored fluids under the car. Be as specific as possible about what you see or feel is wrong with the car, such as you hear a knocking sound in the front left of the car when you turn right, or the car feels like it is pulling to the right when you are on the highway. Make your signoff a requirement. When you take car in, make it clear that you need a phone call with a cost estimate before any work begins. When they tell you what needs to be done and what it will cost, take good notes. Then quickly call three or four other shops and ask what they would charge for the same work. If you don't trust the repair shop, take your car to another shop for a second opinion.

When finally you agree to the work, ask whether the repairs come with a written warranty. Tell them that you would like to keep or at least see your old parts if some parts will be replaced. Before you sign the bill look it over carefully and make sure everything matches up with the estimate you had been given and your notes. If you see anything on the bill that you didn't authorize, speak up. If you need a brake job, ask if the rotors and drums can be resurfaced rather than replaced altogether. If you are told that you have hydraulic system failure, get a second opinion. You can do some online research to see if your mechanic is quoting a fair price at www. RepairPal.com.

Be smart if you get a traffic ticket

Tickets can be expensive. Avoid them by driving within the speed limit, following the rules of the road, practicing courtesy on the road, and not driving while intoxicated, distracted, texting, or otherwise impaired. These common sense behaviors will save you hundreds of dollars in ticket fees, drivers school fees, and increased insurance premiums, not to mention car repairs and medical bills from auto accidents.

If you find yourself driving a bit too fast in your shiny new car, or for some reason are pulled over by a police officer, you can save money on the ticket you might be about to receive with the following tips: pull over carefully right away, turn your car off, roll down your window a few inches and put your hands on the top of your steering wheel. Wait until asked to find your documents. When talking with the officer, don't be comical, don't be overly friendly, and don't be talkative. Be serious and non-committal. Anything you say can be used against you in court. The officer may write down what you say in his notes, which you can request a copy of.

If you don't want to pay the ticket and be punished with higher insurance rates, traffic school may be an option. Shop for the best price. If you go to traffic court and plead non-guilty, have a valid reason. Bring diagrams and photos if at all possible. Dress professionally and act respectfully to the judge and you may have a chance. Your demeanor will be appropriate if you stay focused on how much money you will be saving if you don't have to pay the ticket and the increased insurance rates as a result of the ticket.

Be smart about car rentals

An alternative to buying a car or a second car is renting when you need a car. Here is what you need to know. Hunt for deals and promotional codes online and compare rates at travel websites such as www.Travelocity.com, www.expedia.com, www.priceline.com and www.hotwire.com. When comparing prices, try to match taxes, surcharges and other fees. You may get a better rate if you reserve in advance, especially if you reserve in a low season.

When you reserve the car, get a smaller car. Know exactly when you will be able to return the car or you may pay a late charge. Inquire about weekly rates, which may be lower. Ask about fees such as airport taxes and fees to drop off the car at a different location. Ask if they will block any funds on your credit card. The charge would reduce the spending limit on your credit card.

When you sign the car rental lease, you may be given an option about how to pay for fuel. You will save money if you fill the tank up before you return. Be sure to you save time to do it before you return the car. Ask about the mileage allowance and the charges if you exceed the allowance—whether it is a few cents per mile or a flat fee. Speaking of mileage, if you are planning to take the car across state line, make sure that is allowed.

When you rent a car, you will be given the option to buy insurance. There are three kinds. Collision damage waiver or CDW is insurance that you buy to have the rental car company pay for any damage you may cause to the rental car. Your own auto insurance policy may already cover it, so find out first. Personal accident insurance or PAI pays a death benefit and/or some of your medical bills if you are injured while driving the rental car. Your own life insurance and your own health insurance policies may already cover you, so find out first about this, too. Personal effects coverage or PEC is insurance for your luggage. Your own homeowner's or renter's insurance policy may cover this, so check on that as well.

Before you drive the car off the lot, make sure that you won't have to pay for someone else's damage to the car. Simply bring a camera or your smart phone, turn on the date-and-time option on your camera, walk around the car and take pictures of any dings and dents. Show the photos to the agent and get his or her full name.

Be smart about other ways to save on your car

Here are some more ways to save: Find the cheapest gas in town with sites such as www.GasPriceWatch.com and www.GasBuddy.com. Buy gas at big warehouse stores such as Costco, Sam's Club, BJ's Wholesale Club, Wal-Mart and Kmart. These are things you can do to your car to save gas: Take off car racks and bike racks to reduce wind resistance drag, take out excess weight in your trunk. These are things you can do while driving to save on gas: use cruise control, limit the use of the heater and air conditioning, drive smoothly, drive within the speed limit, pedal lightly, and brake gently. Keep its resale value by keeping it well maintained and looking good. Store it in a garage if possible and hand wash it regularly. Don't let the fuel tank get too low or gunk will get into the fuel system and clog and damage it.

The best way to save on your car is to not have one. Mass transit is always an option. Your employer may provide an incentive to commuting to work on mass transit. You will need to call about a trip planner, be at the correct bus stop or station, ready with the exact change or ticket and sit near the front to be ready to switch to any transfer location. You can join www.Zipcar.com for an annual fee and reserve a car for several dollars per hour. Also check out the new Uber phenomenon, the rideshare and taxi alternative apps, at www.Uber.com and www.Lyft.com.

TRAVEL

"It is not enough to reach for the brass ring.
You must also enjoy the merry-go-round."
—Julie Andrews

WHEN BOOKING WITH A HOTEL for your family, ask if adjoining rooms are available, which is less expensive than two separate rooms. If you like to negotiate on the phone, make one reservation and then call a competitor hotel and tell them that you will switch your reservation to their hotel if they will give you a free night or another type of upgrade.

You and your family can get free breakfasts at many hotels, such as www.EmbassySuites.com and www.HolidayInn.com, www.HamptonInn.hilton.com, and www.ResidenceInn.com

Eat breakfast heartily, and then stop by a local grocery store for the ingredients for a picnic lunch, such as fruit, hard-boiled eggs, crackers, and cheese. If you want to dine out, go to a restaurant for lunch instead of dinner, because the prices are lower but the quality of food is similar. In the evening, there are free happy hours at www.EmbassySuites.com and www.ResidenceInn.com. You can go to a diner and order breakfast, which is lower priced than dinner.

When you check in to the hotel, always ask what free upgrades are available. If you prefer a good view, you may have to give up having a higher floor, but tell them you can be flexible. Remember to pack your discount cards, such as student cards, AAA and AARP, since you may need to show them at check-in to get your discount. Use the free Wi-Fi in the lobby. Don't even touch the minibar, you might be charged a "restocking" fee just for opening the door or moving items around.

Some hotels offer guests free use of a town car within a mileage radius. Speaking of transportation, when you pull up to the entrance of a hotel, ask questions before you hand over the keys to the valet: Is there self-parking? What does it cost compared to valet? What if I am not going to stay overnight. Sometimes, the hotel valet staff will tell you where you can get nearby off-site parking for less. On a recent trip to Monterey, Heidi found out that the hotel valet was $20 per day, but city parking lot was only $4 one block away.

Shop online for the best rates on hotels at www.Octopus-Travel.com, www.HotelClub.com, www.TravelWorm.com and www.HRS.com, in addition to the larger sites www.Hotels.com, and www.Travelocity.com.

If you can be flexible on your dates and destinations, you can bid your way to savings at an auction of certificates for stays at luxury hotels. Check out www.LuxuryLink.com, www.Sky-Auction.com, or www.PriceLine.com. Set a cap that is below the lowest rate that you can find on sites such as www.Kayak.

com. If you are traveling during the weekend, note that hotels in business districts often have lower rates on the weekends.

Be smart about alternatives to hotels

If your family likes to eat a lot and often, you might save money by renting a vacation home (or a hotel with a kitchenette) and cooking meals yourself rather than going to restaurants for every meal. Travel with another family or friends and share gas and expenses such as renting a vacation home. You can also share childcare on the trip and give each set of parents a night off. For vacation home deals, click on www.VacationHomeRentals.com,   www.HomeAway.com, www.VRBO.com, www.Rentalo.com and www.SecondPorch. com. A house right on the beach will cost more than a house a few blocks from the beach. Rent a house a few blocks from the beach and save enough for a car rental.

Consider swapping homes with friends or strangers in different cities. This is the least expensive way to obtain vacation lodging. If you want to pay zero for your lodging in another country, here is the way to do it. Lock up your valuables in a closet and find someone from that country to live in your house for a few days or a few weeks. No-cost house exchanges are great for getting to know a new city or country like a native. It helps if you live in or near a tourist destination area. To get qualified swap partners, you should sign up and pay the annual fee with a home-exchange agency such as www.HomeExchange.com and www.HomeLink.org. These sites will help you find qualified home exchangers, but you should correspond via email for several weeks before you agree and even try to meet briefly to hand over the keys.

Hostels provide safe and clean accommodations at about 80% less than a hotel. Find a list of domestic hotels at www. HIUSA.org. In Europe, see www.HotelWorld.com and www. Hostels.com. Search online for hostel websites in the country of your destination. If you are a veteran or in the military, you can stay at many military bases and military vacation hotels. Another inexpensive lodging option is camping. Book a reservation at a campground at national and state parks at www. ReserveAmerica.com.

If you are comfortable with well-qualified strangers staying in your spare bedroom, or even on your living room sofa, you can find renters by using the www.Airbnb.com service. This company, built on people's willingness to earn extra money by renting out a room, is for real. In its initial three years, it booked more than 5 million nights and became a $1 billion business with more than 100,000 listings available in more than 186 countries.

Or visit www.CouchSurfing.org if you want to meet one of the estimated more than 1.5 million folks who are willing to let you sleep on their couches or spare bedroom for free.

Be smart about airfare

Timing is everything when it comes to airfare. Travel in the off season, generally October through April in Europe. Check out www.CheapTickets.com for a list of when it is least expensive to visit certain destinations domestically and internationally.

Don't wait until the last minute to book your fare. Prices can soar 40% over the average cost if bought on the day of the trip. You get the best price if you buy six weeks before your flight. Domestic flights tend to be lower on Monday night through Wednesdays. Sometimes flights are lower in the early morning and late at night. Check out www.FareCompare.com. Other airfare sites are www.dohop.com, www.AirfareWatchdog.com.

Avoid fees for checked luggage (and the hassle of losing your luggage) by traveling only with a carryon. It is a challenge, so here are some tips for packing light: Pack clothes in only two coordinating colors, select lightweight, layering pieces that can be washed in a sink and dried over the shower rod overnight, pack clothes that work for day and night, and lastly, wear your blazer, overcoat, and heaviest shoes on the plane. If you plan to buy lots of new clothes on your trip, pack old clothes that you are willing to give away on your trip. Have them shipped. Many stores will ship your purchases to a store near your home at no charge.

Be smart about being a tourist

Explore outside of the usual tourist areas. Ask residents in the area, including taxi and bus drivers, about local restaurants that have early-bird specials and all-you-can eat buffets, and children-eat-free specials. Find out if the city has a city card which offers free entry into museums and attractions. These can be purchased online or at local tourism offices. If you are going to Europe, do an online search for European City Cards for discounts in numerous cities.

Contact a regional greeters organization that matches local volunteer "greeters" with tourists, usually a free service. Search online for "greeters" in the area you will be visiting. For example New York City has www.BigAppleGreeter. org and Chicago has www.ChicagoGreeter.com. If you want coupon savings on dining and local attractions for the city you are touring, you can buy an Entertainment Book at www. Entertainment.com.

Try using the local transit systems, buses, metros, and trains. If you need a car during your trip, consider car-sharing websites such as www.ZipCar.com and www.RelayRides.com. You pay a small fee per hour of rental. You can share the entire trip with someone by signing up at www.eRideShare.com and www.ShareYourRide.net. Check out www.AutoSlash.com and www.BreezeNet.com for discounts on car rentals.

Be smart about cruises

Like airfare, timing is the key with cruises. You want to travel with good weather, but you want to get a good deal, too. Avoid holidays and spring or summer break. Instead, cruise right after Labor Day and during the week after Thanksgiving, when everyone is back home after their vacations. The same miss-the-crowd-and-save-some-money approach works for traveling to cities that recently hosted big events. An example is an Olympics host city, which will have lots of open inventory after the games are over.

If you can be flexible, you can save by waiting to book online until the last few days before the ship sets. Also, you can save by using alternative ports such as Charleston, North Carolina; Galveston, Texas; and Norfolk, Virginia.

You can cruise for free and bring a guest if you provide lectures for cruise passengers. Create talks about various destinations, self-help advice, hobbies and skills. Assemble a sales kit with a CD or DVD, letters of recommendation on your speaking skills and a resume about your expertise. Click on www.SpeakerscruiseFree.com, www.SixthStar.com, and www.CompassSpeakers.com.

To save money on cruises, go to www.VacationsToGo.com, www.CruisesOnly.com, www.Cruise.com, www.OnlineVaca-tionCenter.com, and www.CruiseCritic.com.

WEDDINGS

"What other people think of you is none of your business."
—Anonymous

AS WE SAID IN OUR FIRST BOOK, a very nice wedding can be produced for $3,000 to $4,000. For some reason, weddings are getting more expensive when they should be costing less. Make sure that your budget fits with your reality. Remember that it is a ceremony to commit your vows and a celebration of your love, not a coronation. What is it about weddings that causes perfectly reasonable people throw all sense–as well as their life's savings—out the window? It the industry's sales job of what a "perfect" wedding looks like? Is it your family members' dreams? Is it the need to have a wedding that resembles your favorite celebrity? Is it competitiveness with your friends and social circle?

As we wrote in the chapter on weddings in our first book, keep a leash on your dreams. Turn "bridezilla" on her ear. You and your partner can plan a memorable, creative, personalized wedding that is true to who you are and doesn't ruin your financial future. Even in the recession, expenses on weddings have soared. The average wedding costs $27,000— the amount of a car or a down payment on a house. According to one study, more than 70% of couples use savings to pay for their wedding and 30% use credit cards. In this era of outsized, stress-filled weddings, the wedding bills last longer than the marriage.

First choose the wedding location

Pick the location first; then pick the date. Everything else can be decided after that because the location and date set the tone, theme, and budget of the wedding. Try to pick an off-season date, which in wedding terms means a fall wedding in early November, a winter wedding in January or February (not Valentine's Day), or a spring wedding in March or April. Try to avoid the typical summer wedding season months of June, July, September, and October. For significant savings, choose a Monday through Thursday evening. Don't pick a Saturday.

Be creative. For an intimate wedding, you could choose the courtyard of a B&B, the garden of restaurant, a winery patio, a museum garden, a small chapel, or an historic building. For a larger, outdoor wedding there are parks, arboretums, the beach or a lakeside park, a large balcony or a roof top of a tall building that has a great view. An intimate candlelight ceremony can be lovely and doesn't require a large floral budget.

A destination wedding combines the honeymoon with the wedding. Depending on where you plan to go on your honeymoon, this can save you time and money. It also depends on how many guests attend. Search online for a selection of locations and options, including www.sandals.com, which calls their wedding packages "weddingmoons." At some wedding destination resorts, couples are offered a free room if they bring enough guests. Be sure to clarify what you are able to pay for your guests. Some bridal consultants say that the bride and groom should pay for the hotel rooms and food and the guests pay for their own travel expenses.

Be sure that you consult with a wedding planner about the details of obtaining a marriage license if your destination is out of the country. A wedding coordinator can usually add 15% to the cost of a wedding, but in many destination wedding packages include the wedding coordinator. The package should include choice of details such as flowers, music, décor, reception menu, photographer, etc. You and your guest simply arrive, unpack your bags, and enjoy the wedding. You will have less creative options, and probably less privacy, with your guests attending your honeymoon with you. But the time savings and cost-savings can be significant. Some of the cost is defrayed by convenience, which is worthwhile if you don't like to plan big events yourself or if you are short on time

Plan together and maintain harmony

It goes without saying, but it can't be said often enough: for a happy, stress-free wedding that you and your mate will enjoy as much as your guests, you need to plan far, far in advance. First step is the planning phase. Keep the lines of communication wide open at this point, and forever more. Before you make solid plans, sit down with your betrothed and each put your dream list together. List everything that you would love to have. Make sure that you are dreaming of the things that you really want, not just the trappings of a fantasy that the wedding industry wants you to have.

Then each of you will rank your lists by importance. What is more important to you, first-class cuisine—or amazing flowers? An eye-popping dress—or a spectacular location? Unforgettable music—or an unbelievable cake? There will be lots of choices and decisions so that you can stay in your budget and have the wedding you want. Next, compare your lists and begin the first compromise of your soon-to-be-wedded life. Take time to understand what your partner wants and how badly and why. Try to accommodate each other in an innovative way. That way you will both be happy on the first day of your life together. The wedding is not nearly as important as being loving and supportive to each other.

Be sure to keep your list in mind and stay in close communication throughout the planning process so that you are doing planning this event for each other and with each other. The main goal is happy memories for you both, not a "wow" impression for your guests.

Keep the gown in perspective

The largest portion of most wedding budget typically goes to the bride's gown. Remember, this is customarily worn for only one day! Some brides choose a dress that can be worn later as an evening gown, party frock, or dressy suit. A long dress can even be hemmed shorter to wear on more occasions after the wedding. Look in non-bridal stores for white or off-white prom dresses, cocktail dresses, and evening gowns. If you are having a beach wedding, a tea- length chiffon, georgette, crepe, or gauze dress from a department store would be perfect.

If you have a dream dress in mind, here are some ideas that will save money: If you know an excellent seamstress, you can have your one-of-a-kind dress made for you. If you won't settle for anything but a designer gown, you can rent one at sites like www.OneNightAffair.com. Look for discounts on dresses and accessories at www.yesbride.com. The website www.net-a-porter.com has more affordable designer gowns. Retailers are getting into the bridal business, too, such as Anne Taylor, Chico's, J. Crew and even Urban Outfitters have a bridal line. You can buy a pre-owned dress at www.oncewed.com, www.BravoBride.com, www.PreownedWeddingDresses.com, and www.SmartBrideBoutique.com. Also check www.craigslist.com and www.ebay.com. Look in the phone book for a bridal shop that rents gowns.

Wear silk flowers or a floral wreath or a rhinestone pin in your hair instead of an expensive veil that you will never wear again. If you must have a veil, first decide how you will wear your hair and then try on lots of veils with that hairdo. You can buy books on making veils or buy a bridal veil kit at a craft stores. They also provide veiling which has already been cut and gathered and ready to attach to a headpiece or a comb you can decorate yourself with gems and a glue gun or silk flowers. Jewelry can get expensive, so if you absolutely must wear a dazzling piece, consider renting it at www.Adorn-Brides.com.

Buy your shoes at a regular store during the spring and summer, when white, off-white and pastel shoes are available. Wear them frequently before the wedding to break them in. If you are having a garden wedding or will be walking on grass, remember that narrow heels will sink into the ground. Opt instead for a more comfortable, wider-based heel. If you are wearing a long full dress, your shoes will seldom be seen, so wear low comfortable heels in silver or gold. You can embellish your own shoes with fabric glue and sequins, beads, rhinestones, pearls, flowers, lace, ribbons.

For the bridal bouquet, the easiest and least expensive is silk flowers, which can be prepared in advance. The flowers, greenery, and ribbons can be purchased in the exact colors on sale at a crafts store. If you want fresh, create your own, with a single long-stem lily, rose, or amaryllis or a bunch of flowers wrapped with floral tape and wide ribbon.

Decide what everyone else will wear

Your bridesmaids and maid of honor are women that you care about. Show them by letting them participate in the decision of the dress that you are going to ask them to wear at your wedding. They will appreciate your consideration.

Allow for some variety and you will help everyone save money. They may already own nice black evening dresses that would work for your theme, especially if you have a black and white, a black and gold, a black and silver, or a black and bronze color theme. They could wear black dresses that they already have and you could add lame wraps with the metallic color of your choice—gold, silver or bronze. If your bridesmaids want to buy new dresses, they can find nice ones at a discount at a non-bridal store, and avoid the "wedding markup."

You can also be creative with the groom's attire. Why not buy a nice suit that he can wear the rest of his life? For a casual wedding, the groom and his groomsmen could all wear silk floral shirts or solid dress shirts in pastel colors with handmade floral ties that coordinate with the bridesmaids' dresses. Boutonnieres are usually flower that is the same as a flower in the bride's bouquet. Just cut the stem to about three inches, wrap with floral tape and pin it with a pearl head pin.

Keep everything special, but not expensive

We mentioned lots of great ideas about weddings in our first book *TheSmartestWay™ to Save.* For your shower, choose a practical theme such as kitchen, or linens, or gardening that will help you with getting your new home set up or a hobby that you both share.

You can make your invitations yourself with self-printed kits from www.invitesite.com, www.AnnsBridalBargain.com and craft stores such as Michaels www.Michaels.com, Hobby Lobby www.HobbyLobby.com, and Party City www.PartyCity.com. If you have a big wedding, you will save money on postage by inserting reply postcards instead of reply cards and envelopes. You can email invitations to showers and bachelorette/bachelor's parties.

Think about how much money you want to spend on your rings. Jewelry has a huge markup, sometimes 300% or more. Don't be bashful about asking for a big discount. You may get a further price reduction if you pay in cash. The monetary value of wedding rings is vastly overrated. A wedding ring is a symbol of your commitment to each other: it is not a symbol of your status. Therefore, if you need to choose, it shouldn't be a substitute for a down payment on your dreams such as a home. A wedding ring doesn't have to be expensive to be meaningful, symbolic, sentimental, and emotionally valuable. Talk it out, share your feelings, dreams and plans and buy your rings accordingly.

Be open to creative and beautiful options for your rings. Try vintage clothing shops and vintage jewelry stores and estate sales for vintage rings. Consider diamond alternatives. There are many other beautiful stones and they all look wonderful with diamond accents. If you are selecting a significant diamond, do your research on the carat weight, clarity, color, cut and cost of diamonds. An attractive but economical alternative to diamonds are lab-created diamonds. They are many gems besides real diamonds than cubic zirconium, but cost much less than real diamonds.

For decoration of the wedding location, try www.Oriental-Trading.com for tulle or satin pew bows, table coverings, ring bearers pillow, flower girl's basket, guest book, cake knife, and personalized champagne glasses. Silk flowers are great for pew decorations and for decorating arbors, especially if the weather is warm. For entertainment on a back wall, you could project a slide show of photos of the couple together. You can bring the decorations from the ceremony to the reception. Costco has a nice floral department. Talk to the floral manager at Costco or Sam's Club.

A wedding program can be made from programs available online. This can include the order of the service, explanations about certain music or parts of the ceremony, poetry or song lyrics, quotes and thank you essays.

Choose the right photographer and music

Ask at the local college for a recommendation of a talented student. Or hire a professional one to get the great posed shots, during the wedding. They will do a better job than a well-meaning friend or relative who may get lost in the moment of the ceremony. But put a limit on the package and the number of hours for the professional photographer. When comparing bids, ask for comparable packages. If possible, choose a photographer who provides negatives so you can make your own copies and enlargements. Ask friends and relatives to promise that they will take lots of candid shots with disposable cameras. Assign a responsible relative to collect the cameras for you.

For the ceremony, often a church will have an organist, pianist, and/or vocalist that charges a reasonable fee. If you are not near an organ or piano, remember that a harpist, flutist, violinist or a small chamber orchestra can travel almost anywhere. Don't forget to check with the local college's music department. If you are booking a band for the reception, ask if one or two of the band members can also provide music or vocals at the wedding at a nominal cost. If your wedding is in the afternoon, ask for a discount, since they will be able to book another function that evening.

Have a reasonable gift registry

A registry is a good idea because it cuts down on the number of redundant gifts. Choose a store that has a wide variety of products you actually need, such Target, Wal-Mart, or Bed Bath & Beyond. Offer a registry of big items such as a guest can sponsor the limo or the flowers or the flight for your honeymoon. You can mention the thank you for these items in the wedding program, if you have one. Register for a number of items in a broad price range, so there is something that everyone can afford, from $25 to $150. Mention the registry tastefully in an extra slip of paper in the invitation: "For your convenience, we have a gift registry at Target." You can mention your registry and share other details of your wedding on your own wedding website. You can create a personalized one for free at www.ewedding.com.

Plan a memorable reception

Make your reception special by picking an unusual location and a special theme. You could have a western theme with a barbeque in a barn with a fiddling band, an elegant Manhattan theme with a dessert buffet in a museum with a harpist, a Victorian theme with high tea in historic estate with a small chamber orchestra, a Camelot theme with a fancy picnic in a wooded glen with a flutist, an Italian theme with a wine tasting with cheese, fruit, crackers and a jazz combo in a vineyard.

Ask friends if they can help if they have a home overlooking a lake or the seaside, or are members of a country club. Perhaps you have a friend who would be glad to drive you to the reception in their luxury car or vintage car. Ask for help and accept offers of help. Say, "Yes, thank you!" to anyone who is qualified to make your big day a little easier or a little less expensive.

Economize by borrowing tables and chairs from a friend or club and using clear plastic disposable plates, cups and cutlery. If neither you, your partner, nor your friends love dancing, skip the expense of a DJ, band, or a dance floor. Instead, you can make your own playlist of your favorite songs based on your theme, and hook up your iPod to a borrowed sound system.

The caterer doesn't have to be at the reception or serve the food. You could have "drop off" catering, where the caterer delivers and sets up a buffet of already prepared food. Ethnic food is plentiful and less expensive. If it is a brunch shower or morning wedding, serve mimosas, which can be inexpensive champagne and orange juice. Ask a local winery if they would be willing to do a wine tasting at your wedding and give you a few cases at a discount in exchange.

In hard economic times, sometimes reception venues go out of business. Keep an eye open for warning signs such as super deep discounts, poor customer service, recent staff reductions. Have a backup location in mind, just in case. If you have concerns about disreputable vendors, damaged gifts or gowns, injury, illness, or even unreliable weather, you can buy wedding insurance from companies such as www.WedSafe. com. The National Alliance of Special Event Planners provides insurance that will even cover cold feet, at very reasonable rates.

Decorate the table with centerpieces and favors

There are many ways to decorate the reception tables, depending on the theme of the reception. For an autumn wedding you could have fall leaves, gold-painted acorns, sunflowers and raffia bows. The place cards could be held by tiny pumpkins. For a spring wedding you could have small terra-cotta pots with herbs and flower seed packets. Some favors could also serve as place cards if you have sit-down dinner. Frosted fruit in a glass container or baskets is inexpensive and easy for a reusable centerpiece. To make frosted fruit: Use strawberries, figs pears, plums, grapes, lemons limes, berries, cherries, etc. Paint the fruit with a pastry brush dipped in beaten egg whites. Immediately sprinkle fruit all over with sugar. Keep refrigerated. When buying in bulk, always ask for a quantity discount.

Big Lots stores www.biglots.com and Smart and Final stores www.smartandfinal.com are good places to look for table cloths. IKEA www.ikea.com has lots of candles and imaginative centerpiece holders. You can find used wedding items are at www.tradesy.com/weddings. You could use plants or flowering bulbs in pretty pots or baskets. The guests at each table can be encouraged to play an icebreaker game and the winner takes home the centerpiece. Or ask someone to deliver the centerpieces to a retirement home or hospital after the wedding. If it is a spring wedding and your colors are the fruity colors of spring, consider centerpieces of glass bowls filled with lemons, limes, strawberries, and a few daisies. Display your favors on a cake plate as centerpiece.

For a summer wedding in a warm location, inexpensive hand fans could be a welcome favor. Spray paint them in your wedding colors. If you have an Asian theme, you could give decorated chopsticks tied with a bow. Other inexpensive, do-it-yourself favors are CDs featuring your favorite songs, picture frames with your favorite quote, or homemade barbeque sauce, chutney, or herb-infused oils in bottles from a dollar store. Decorate favors with ribbon from the dollar store and a handmade tag. Remember to save some favors to give as gifts to those who were not able to attend. For your wedding scrapbook, save a copy of the invitation, the menu, your vows, plus ribbons, boutonnieres, flower petals.

Go on a relaxing honeymoon

There is a lot of controversy about the new practice of asking for financial help with the honeymoon as a wedding gift. Some guests may resist the idea of being asked for money, so get the recommendations of those you trust. It is a risky idea to count on other people to fund your honeymoon. Have a quick alternative plan, in case a situation arises to change your honeymoon plans. If all this fuss and planning is just too much for you, the least expensive wedding is no wedding. Before you plan to elope, be sure to research the legal requirements of marriage (Las Vegas is one of the easiest locations). Plan a nice reception when you get home.

When planning your honeymoon, let the hotel know that you are on your honeymoon. You may get upgrades. Also, at restaurants, nightclubs and shows, announce your honeymoon status. Don't cram your honeymoon full of expensive sight-seeing and social events. The purpose of a honeymoon is to relax and enjoy your time together, so schedule lots of downtime. The simple, romantic, intimate times together are the ones you remember the most about a honeymoon—not the ones where you spent the most money.

Illustration by Ros Webb

"Honey, when do you want to start worrying about how we are going to pay the mortgage this month?"

Chapter 2

MANAGE YOUR RESIDENCE

"Buy land. They ain't making any more of the stuff."
—Will Rogers

WE SAVED the "biggest thing in life" for the last chapter. Typically, where you live will require the largest total expense of your lifetime.

Sam is often asked which is more important, saving or investing. He says, "This is a great question, and as a graduate of Stanford Law School, I answer in the typical lawyer fashion, 'It depends'." Saving on large items is often most important. As we said in Chapter 9, 80% of savings will result from a few proper choices in large matters, such as where you choose to live, the kind of transportation you select, the school your children go to and clothing you buy. As we also have already said, it would take eliminating decades of daily Starbucks visits to save as much money as you can in just a single decision on where to live.

To buy or not to buy a home

This decision is one of those large, "life changing" decisions. Once you sign on the dotted line to buy a home, there is no going back. It could be the best financial decision you ever make, or one you regret for years. You have to look at the timing. Is this the right time in your life to make a change and a commitment? For example, we suggest that if you recently started a new job, wait a few months at least to find out if everything is going to run smoothly at your new job. If you want to fix your credit rating, you may need to rent for awhile first and make sure that you can pay all your bills and pay down all of your credit cards. If you are dealing with a health crisis, you may not have the focus and stamina right now that is required to buy and get settled in a new home. You may want to wait until you are in a stronger position with your health and finances.

While your stage in life is important, also is the status of the real estate market in your area. You may be ready to buy, but the market may not be ready. To analyze the situation, do some serious research online and by interviewing realtors and others who have a good sense of the local market. Don't depend only on what you read in the local or national newspapers. In other words, don't make one of the biggest financial decisions of your life based on a headline. Real estate developments are fostered in micro-economies. What is true for one neighborhood could be false for another neighborhood nearby.

Buying versus renting a home

The decision on whether to rent or buy comes down to money. In general, you should not spend more than 28%-30% of after-tax income on where you live.

In many of smaller towns throughout the United States there is not much difference in cost between monthly rent and a mortgage. Nevertheless, more people are renting their homes these days and there are a number of reasons why.

Americans are becoming used to renting the good life. They know what they like and they want it at a reduced price. It started with renting luxury cars and has developed into a trend to rent luxury homes. During the housing boom, the homeownership rate grew steadily. But since the housing bust, the rentership and its social acceptance has grown.

Renting is easier, with less responsibility and liability. If something breaks, you can require the landlord to repair it. It is usually less expensive on a monthly basis and you don't have to tie up your funds in a down payment. But you don't build equity, which you would if you were paying a mortgage. Also, you may have limited privacy, freedom, and may have limitations on lifestyle issues such as pets. You also are subject to your landlord's change of rules or rent increases. If the landlord decided to make your apartment into a condo, you would be forced to either buy the apartment or move.

With your own home, you have more rights, privacy, and freedom. You can build fences, remodel, and use your favorite color of paint. It adds to your equity, your investment portfolio, and you can deduct the interest paid on your mortgage when you pay your federal income taxes. With ownership, you call the shots. If you buy, you have a widely held consensus that real estate will appreciate, eventually. You just have to estimate how much time you have to wait for your home to build equity. Maybe it will take too long for your plans. On the other hand, maybe in your area of the country, there is no time to wait, and the best time to buy is now.

If you are on the fence about buying versus renting, you can find some free, online rent-to-buy calculators. One is www.trulia.com, which has an index based on the country's fifty largest cities. The ratio is determined by multiplying rent times 12 months and dividing that figure into the average home price. A low ratio means you will save money by owning, a high ratio means you will save money by renting.

Pre-planning will save you money

When shopping for a home, you will get a better deal and save money if you are ready to buy as soon as the right home comes on the market. Do your house-buying home-work. Before you start looking, find out the amount of loan you can afford. Get an official letter from your lender that verifies your loan availability. Then you will be looking at the right homes. Second, find the areas in which you are willing to live. Third, make an extensive list of the specific features you need and want in the home you seek. Fourth, ask a realtor to show you homes with your specifications. Fifth, walk through as many houses as possible. This will help you adjust your list of needs and wants.

Another aspect of your timing is the season. During certain times of the year different neighborhoods may be less expensive. For example, an area that has a reputa-tion for great schools may have higher home prices at the beginning of summer, when families are looking to make a move while their kids are not in school. Not many are looking for homes during the busy time of December holidays, so you may find a more willing seller then.

Remember all the hidden expenses

As with the cost of any large item, before you decide to buy a house, you must first know what the true cost is, can you afford it, and what can you do as an alternative? As we explained in our first book *TheSmartestWay™ to Save—Why You Can't Hang Onto Money and What To Do About It,* to spend a dollar you must earn a dollar sixty. Therefore to make a $100,000 down payment you have to earn $160,000. In determining the true cost of buying a home, much more than the purchase price must be considered.

Operating costs will include utilities, property taxes, property insurance, repairs, maintenance, and the loss of income on the equity invested, in addition to the interest and principal on your mortgage. Get property insurance and make sure you have enough. Saving money by being under-insured can be an expensive bet. Theft and damage without sufficient coverage can cost you much more than the coverage. Upgrade your liability coverage and get an umbrella policy for extra protection, if needed. Find out what is the full replacement cost of your home, which is the estimated cost to rebuild, not just the actual value. Standard policies don't usually cover floods, earthquakes or sewer backups. If you have a lot of collectibles or valuables, you can buy an extra rider.

While owning a home can provide a great deal of personal satisfaction, many do not carefully calculate exactly what home ownership costs. Don't forget to add flood insurance and earthquake insurance where needed. Each home you look at, ask what is the average cost of the monthly electricity, gas, water, sewer, and trash removal services? Does the house require a monthly water softener system maintenance? A big expense can be home association dues. Your realtor is required to disclose this amount. Don't forget to add, realistically, the cost of extra furnishings, flooring, appliances, window coverings, and any remodeling that is required right away. Get inspections of all mechanical systems and structures on hill side, which may have geological and other conditions as well.

The best choice for your first home is a good, solid neighborhood with good public schools. If you buy a home in an expensive neighborhood, remember that everything in your new neighborhood will cost more, including groceries, medications, basic services, gas, and repairs. Also, your taxes will be higher. When you go out to eat, your restaurant and entertainment costs will be greater. You may want to send your children to private school. Your children's friends may spend more on their wants and needs. All these factor should be entered into your calculations.

Talk to your advisors first

Estimate how much the home would appreciate. Also take a hard look at mortgage rates and how easy will it be for you to obtain a loan. These are questions for a good realtor and mortgage lender, as well as your banker and CPA or accountant. Take the tax benefits of ownership into consideration. As of the publication of this book, you can deduct the annual mortgage interest on the first million dollars of acquisition debt and the property taxes if you own your home. Congress keeps talking about tinkering with these crucial deductions, so don't count on them lasting forever. Estimate as exactly as possible the amount you would save each year with this deduction. The mortgage tax deduction gives a slight break if you itemize your deductions.

As part of your decision to buy a home, you may consider the appreciation, or the increasing value of that home over time. Nevertheless, don't over-rely on the value of the home rising quickly. Also, don't over-estimate the amount that it will increase in value. Current estimates are that your home may appreciate in value over the next ten years. But don't decide to buy a house solely because you want it to become an equity bank. Those days may be over. If you are planning to sell within a certain period, remember that when you do sell, you will have to pay broker commissions, which will consume some of your profit.

Among other costs in purchasing a home (as most of us will be financing the home) is the cost of securing the mortgage which can include points, service charges, and fees. These will often be as much as 1 to 1.5% of the loan therefore a $300,000 loan will add $3,000 to $4,500 at the front end on the cost of the house. There will be escrow charges and title insurance fees. In some County's the practice is for the Buyer to pay for the title insurance and in others the Seller. Depending on how property taxes are figured there may be property taxes and other items to be advanced as impounds in connection with the loan. In most markets the brokerage fee on a sale will be paid by the Seller if real estate brokers are involved.

In some cases the transaction may require the services of an attorney. Hire someone other than the one recommended by the Seller or the Seller's broker. In hiring an attorney endeavor to find one with experience in real estate who is familiar with all the local forms and practices, and who will represent you in the transaction for a flat fee. If you are going to do so add that to your estimate of the cost of purchase of the house. If you are not going to hire an attorney you might want to get a good book on the subject of buying your own home. See the biography attached for suggestions.

Do all your house-hunting research

Spend some time getting to know the neighborhood and the prices for homes that meet your needs. It is often said that 90% of the homes will be priced at fair comparable prices. About 5% of the homes in the multiple listing will be at or below the current market value because the seller is highly motivated due to divorce, relocation, or downsizing. Another 5% will be substantially above the market value. It is worth the time to comparison shop to find a house that costs 5% to 10% below comparable houses. Look for a home that meets your needs, is in good condition, and needs few if any repairs or rehabilitation.

When you find it, be ready to put it under contract quickly, or someone else will take it within a few days. If you can find a true bargain that meet all of the above criteria keep in mind that if you are purchasing with 20%

down and you save 10% of the value of the house, you've saved 50% of your equity. If you are going to sell within a relatively short period of time say five years for you to gain anything on the house it would have to increase more than 6 to 8% to cover brokerage and closing cost on the resale.

If you are struggling to afford a house, do some research on anti-poverty programs such as EARN. Launched in San Francisco in 2001, it is one of hundreds of organizations that offer Individual Development Accounts. These are special savings accounts that offer to match your funds, in other words, double the amount that you put into the savings account. A nonprofit organization called Corporation for Enterprise Development www.cfed.org can help you with the search.

Estimate remodeling costs

Don't over invest in remodeling your house. If it is "over remodeled" you may not recoup those expenses when you sell. Sometimes an unplanned sale is required in order to stay afloat financially, due to those devastating D's—divorce, disability, disease, death, default, downsizing at the office, etc.

Most remodeling projects take an average of twice as much time and twice as much cost as originally estimated. Sam says it is one of Murphy's Sub Laws. What adds more value to the home is to increase the living space, either by room additions, rehabbing the attic or basement, or adding a deck, porch, side patio, or balcony. A mid-range kitchen or bathroom remodel is an investment you will recoup more than an upscale facelift.

Here are some more things to watch out for. Beware if the contractor or seller says you don't need a permit. Don't be persuaded by a contractor to go with a cost-plus" contract, one that calls for the owner to pay the contractor's costs plus a percentage for overhead and profit ranging from 8% to 25%. Instead bargain for a "fixed-price" contact. Make sure that the contract states precisely and entirely what you have agreed on. Include specifics on materials and timelines and payment schedule. Pay the contractor only when each work phase is completed. Depending on the size of the project, you may need to hire a project manager.

There are many ways to save on remodeling expenses, and as with any other purchase, you should focus on value and utility. There's a long list of things that can be done to provide form, function and appearance, by using alternate high-quality materials. Laminate floors which look like wood will last longer, maintain their appearance better, and are often half or less the cost of natural wood. They are also less subject to mold, warping, and in some cases, fire. There are also a number of composite materials available that have the appearance of granite, stone, or other hard surfaces that may be more durable, equally attractive, and in some cases, almost indistinguishable from natural stone. Some of these materials are available at a fraction of the cost of natural stone.

Consider the schools in your target area

One of the biggest family expenses can be private school tuition. Carefully consider a neighborhood with a good public school system, which can save you, during the 12 years that your children are in elementary and high school, $5,000 - $30,000 per child, per year. You will save much more in a neighborhood where you are comfortable with the public school system and know that your children are getting a proper education in a good public school. A home which is adequate but not bigger than you need, in such a neighborhood, will cost less in insurance, taxes, maintenance and utilities than one in a fancier area.

Several websites, such as www.GreatSchools.org, rate school test scores and reviews of the schools in the area you are considering. First do your online research and then do your boots-on-the-ground research of talking with families who live in the area and actually doing onsite visits at the schools and interviewing the staff. A local realtor also should have the ratings and information on the local school system for both the immediate neighborhood you prefer as well as surrounding areas.

While a neighborhood may appear to be expensive if you have young children who will be in school for a considerable length of time you often will find buying a more expensive small house in a better school district to be more advantageous, rather than buying a house in an area where you feel your children must get their education outside the public school system.

Sam recalls a young woman who consulted him about purchasing a condominium on the west side of Los Angeles. At the time he identified a motivated seller who would sell a two bedroom, two bath condominium in a neighborhood with an excellent school system (a good resale prospect) and could be purchased for $600,000. She had available about $350,000 for down payment and while she made substantial money, she had been through several jobs in the recent past. Her income could support servicing debt up to $650,000 and she brought a luxury high-end condominium with a concierge, doorman etc., using her resources for the down payment.

When she lost her high paying job and the market collapsed, the condominium was in an area that did not have a public school system as good as the one where the lower priced condominium was, and she could not resell the one she bought for more than the debt losing her $350,000 down payment. If she had purchase the other condominium her payments on $250,000 rather than

$650,000 would have been sufficient for her newer much lower paying job to cover and she would still have her own home.

Consider whether to sell your home

All real estate is local. Whether to sell and when to sell depends on many factors. Talk to a realtor about the price he or she thinks you could get for your house currently and future projections. If you need to downsize to save money, look at all the ramifications. There may be push-back from family members or friends. There will be unexpected expenses. There will be an adjustment period. But sometimes you've got to do what you've got to do. The money you put in your pocket is considered a "windfall," which means you don't spend it on wants. Use it for investment or emergency reserves.

Perhaps you need to help an elderly relative make a move. Plan carefully and engage all the family members and all available local resources. A coordinated effort will help guard against you ending up holding the bag for all of the expenses.

If you decide to sell your house, find an excellent realtor who can tell you what you need to do to your house to prepare it for sale. If you do it right, you will spend a little but get more back in a higher sales price. Some of the preparation for house-selling only requires what Heidi's mother calls "elbow grease." No-cost/low-cost tasks are:

1. de-cluttering—to remove all personal items, organize closets and shelves;
2. cleaning—including windows to make the house light and bright;
3. eliminating—old shabby drapes and carpets;
4. gardening—trimming trees and shrubbery, laying in colorful flowers and bark;

5. repairing—fixing leaks, lights, and outlets; and

6. painting—a fresh coat of neutral-colored paint.

More expensive projects include upgrading the kitchen with appliances that match in brand and color and buffing up the bathrooms. Just remember, don't overdo it. Instead, save your money for investing in your new home.

When you sell your home for a higher dollar amount than you bought it for, look at the gain realistically. There is something called "money illusion," which occurs when you think in terms of nominal values rather than real values. You need to think of money in terms of its actual purchasing power rather than its face value. Remember your home upgrade expenses over the duration of owning the home. Remember the erosion power of inflation. These will help you more realistically assess how much "extra" money you actually made when you sold your home.

Use financial clarity in a divorce

One of the many devastating results of divorce is that when home-owning couples divorce, they often sell their home and end up living in apartments the rest of their lives. Their divorce resulted in them both losing the best financial investment of their lives. Nevertheless, divorce may necessitate downsizing. Not understanding the financial obligations of maintaining a house may cause eventual hardship on the spouse that elects to keep the house in a divorce. Often times, one spouse will have been the "saver" and the other spouse was the "spender." In a divorce, this becomes clear as each one is now on their own. Before you choose to remain in the original home, sit down with an accountant or CPA and estimate all the maintenance expenses.

If your ex is keeping the house, you may still be liable for the payments even if you no longer live there. Don't let your name be taken off the title without getting your name off the mortgage. Your ex should refinance in his or her name, so you won't be on the hook if payments become delinquent.

Your choice is a lasting and major one: can you afford to keep the house? Will it continue to be where you want and need to live? How much and how fast will your investment appreciate? Or will the house become a financial ball-and-chain that prevents you from taking on new opportunities in a new location, a new lifestyle, a new relationship? Only you can know.

Reconsider paying off your home

Conventional wisdom says that the sooner you get your mortgage paid off, the sooner you quit paying interest on the loan. That's true, but there are other considerations that are often overlooked. And remember, making extra payments doesn't reduce the interest rate on the mortgage. It just reduces the amount of time you will be making payments and therefore the amount of interest you end up paying. This assumes that you won't sell the home or refinance before the mortgage is paid off.

Some advisors suggest taking a long-term, fixed-rate mortgage typically 30 years, as interest rates may rise. If you pay off your mortgage faster than necessary, you are giving the bank money sooner and therefore you can't use that money for other investments that may have a higher rate of return. This is also called lack of liquidity; the money is non-liquid because it is now owned by the bank. Every dollar you give to the bank is one that you will never get back until you sell your home. Consider that you may need that money if you lose your job, get sick or disabled.

When interest rates are so low, you can keep the home loan and invest spare money somewhere else at a better interest rate. For example, if you are carrying credit card debt, pay that off first because the interest rate is higher and the interest on credit cards is not tax deductible. Make sure that you have a healthy savings account. Make sure that your retirement accounts are maxed out. Whatever you do, don't use your retirement funds to pay off your house. You will owe income taxes on it and you would lose the opportunity for those funds to grow tax-deferred.

Be cautious about reverse mortgages

If you have equity in your house and you cannot obtain an equity line of credit, you may find yourself considering a reverse mortgage. A reverse mortgage simply defined is a loan against your home equity that you don't have to pay back as long as you live in your home. The equity makes the monthly mortgage payments.

Nevertheless, you could still lose your home. You could default and lose your home if you fall behind on your property taxes, homeowner's insurance, homeowner-association fees, or don't maintain your home property. As of March 2010, the federal government reports, more than 20,0000 reverse-mortgage borrowers were in default. These loans can be expensive. They have upfront fees and annual insurance premiums. There are closing costs associated with setting up a reverse mortgage, even if the line of credit is never tapped. Besides, no matter what you call it, it is still a loan.

You may think that you are going to stay in your home for the rest of your life, but life has an interesting way of changing when you aren't looking. Before you decide, do your research on the best deal and talk with your CPA and an elder-law attorney.

Save on furniture and decorating

Collect ideas by reading magazines and searching the Internet. Do your comparison shopping on the Internet, too. For good deals on furniture, check out Goodwill, Salvation Army www.Freecycle.org, www.Free-Share.org, Costco www.costco.com and Sam's Club www.SamsClub. com. Furniture typically goes on sale December through January and then again in May through August. Consider the transportation cost of delivering the furniture piece to your home. If the piece will be enduring years of hard use, make sure it has sturdy construction. If you won't be using it that long or that hard, it doesn't have to be top quality. Pay for only the level of quality that you need. Make sure all contracts and guarantees have everything in writing. Get out your tape measure and graph paper to be sure it will all fit before you buy. If you buy something at IKEA, which has a discount section, be sure you have all the necessary tools to construct it.

To decorate your new home, you don't have to spend a lot on art. You can buy a large coffee table book of black and white art pictures and frame them with inexpensive black or white frames. Also, look for hotel and rental furniture outlets for durable, attractive, and discounted furniture.

Save on utility bills

We offer lots of ideas on saving on your utilities in our first book. More states are offering incentives to install solar panels, so ask your local hardware store and search for information online. The twisty CFL (compact fluorescent Light) bulbs have received the limelight. Their big drawback is that they contain small amounts of mercury and have to be handled carefully when they burn out and if they break. Unplug appliances when not in use. The Department of Energy estimates that "vampire" power is responsible for 5 percent of the total energy used, totaling $3 billion. Vampires include plasma screen televisions, swimming pool heaters, and floor space heaters and fans.

Use heavy draperies that keep the sun and heat out in the summer and keeps the cold and drafts out in the winter. You can also add reflective window tint or hand inexpensive pull-down blinds or bamboo shades outside. Attic insulation can save up to twenty-five percent on heating and cooling costs. Close your chimney flue damper when not in use to prevent hot or cold air from swooping down the chimney. Reduce the use of your kitchen exhaust fan and your bathroom fans. They pull the warm air out of your house. A faucet dripping a drop every second wastes 192 gallons per month. Leaky faucets drip about 3,000 gallons of water a year. You can insulate your water heater in a pre-cut jacket for less than $20. Set your automatic sprinklers to run during the early morning rather than in the heat of the day. Put mulch around plant roots to help the soil retain water. Find alternatives to grass, such as realistic-looking fake grass, pea gravel, decomposed granite, river rock accents, and drought-resistant ground covers. You can also use pavers, flagstone, and bricks. Less grass means less water usage and less time and money you spend mowing, weeding, and trimming. Check out www.xeriscape.sustainablesources.com

Make extra money with your home

There are many ways to make your home make money for you. Here are just a few suggestions: Do you pay for a gym membership? How about canceling it and making a spare bedroom or a corner of the garage into a gym? If you like to teach aerobics, yoga, or meditation classes, you might even find space in your home to teach them. Heidi has had friends who hold small classes in their homes, teaching yoga and or giving small mastermind trainings in special skills such as color analysis. Another friend conducts art and painting classes for the children in her neighborhood. Do you rent an office space? Maybe you can set up your office in your home, as long as it is quiet enough to prevent constant distractions. Do you spend a lot of time and latte money at the local coffee shop because you just need a quiet place to relax? Maybe you could create a mini-sanctuary in your own home and save the time and expense of going out. Perhaps there is a little reading and meditation nook in your home or bedroom.

If you love to meet people and cook for them, you could consider an old-fashioned concept, taking in boarders. In your area, there could be a need for home-like residences for camp counselors or college students. If they are young, their parents may appreciate an adult on the premises to provide a bit of supervision, versus them living in an apartment on their own. By making your home into a boarding house, you would be providing daily meals to your boarders, but this might be a way to bring in extra money and add to your social life and build an "extended family" at the same time.

Be a wise landlord

Another way to make money on your home is to rent out a room. Before you decide to rent out a room in your home, do your research and decide if it is legal, is it practical, and is it desirable.

1. Is it legal? Check with your zoning board or an attorney experienced in these matters. You may need to file a formal application. To be found in violation of zoning laws is an expensive entanglement.
2. Is it practical? There may be some significant remodeling costs necessary to prepare your house for a renter, such as building an additional exit door.
3. Is it desirable? Make sure you are willing to change your lifestyle and give up some of your privacy. Your duties as a landlord will require a learning curve and some time.

Speaking of being desirable, is your home going to be attractive to potential renters? If the answers to all these questions is yes, you may be on your way to a lucrative experience as a landlord.

If you decide to rent a room in your home, treat your position as a landlord with professionalism. Before your advertise for renters, check with your owners or condominium association to make sure your allowed to rent out a room in your home. Interview renter prospects in person. Check them out thoroughly. A real estate agent or your bank can run a credit check. Confirm their rental history, including recommendations from the last two renters. Confirm their employment history by calling their employers for the last two years at least. The rule of thumb is that monthly income should be four times the monthly rent. Have a formal contract. The lease should be short-term, so you have an exit strategy if the renter doesn't work out, perhaps only on a month-to-month basis. Include all the details, such as who pays utilities, where everyone parks their cars, and whether kitchen privileges and overnight guests, smoking, and/or drinking are permitted.

Sam has all potential employees' screened by obtaining their credit reports and background checks. You should do the same when you take in a tenant. It is worth the extra effort and expense to protect yourself. By spending a little extra time and money, you will save on making up potentially missed payments. A qualified, reliable tenant who rents from you long term is worth the effort.

Three types of renters

Now there are three types of renters in this real estate economy. The first group can afford to buy a home but are renting by choice. They may decide to never own a home because they want the ease of no maintenance or repairs. They like the flexibility that they can simply move by giving one month's notice. They may be reluctant to commit the down payment on a home in a down economy. They may be using the funds instead on starting a new business. They may be working through divorce or relocation or just sitting on the sidelines figuring out exactly where they want to live and what is happening in the housing market that they choose.

The second group is made up of former home-owners who lost their homes in a housing crisis. They are more likely to rent from property owners than from apartment complexes, which tend to place more emphasis on credit history. They are saving their money and repairing their credit by paying everything on time, in order to someday buy another home.

The third group is the adult offspring of the second group. These young adults saw their parents get walloped by the bursting housing bubble. There's a massive loss of wealth in the middle class through loss in housing equity, in which most middle class wealth resides. Also, young people are saddled with the most enormous college debt in history. They may choose the flexibility and variety of renting, over the stability and commitment of homeownership. They are also having trouble finding jobs to help them pay for those student loans. They may want better neighborhoods and cultural attractions but not be able to afford to buy there, so they rent instead. They are reframing the notion that owning a home is the American dream.

Counterbalancing the trend to rent is a trend for middle-aged single women with high incomes to decide to "settle down" on their own and to buy a home. They are far outnumbering the number of single males who are buying their homes. This may seem like an empowering move for these women, as long as the investment is sound financially. Home buying is a major and complex financial investment.

It may be give a sense of empowerment, but it will not give a sense of liberation, due to the fact that home ownership is an obligation that should not be made for mainly emotional reasons or because that is what a grown woman "should" do. All adults, whether male or female, have to make careful decisions about what is right specifically for them. You have to know that you will be staying in your job and your neighborhood for the long-term.

Thinking big in small spaces

Apartment living in a newly renovated location may offer smaller spaces, but more luxury than a purchased house. House sizes have gotten smaller, too. Stores like IKEA are popular with shoppers who like to wander through the floor models of complete apartments stylishly designed in 300-to 500-foot spaces. Ideas abound there about how to use your limited floor space and wall space efficiently but attractively. Use graph paper to map the room to figure out what furniture will fit. The no-cost option of a punch of bold color will add style and durability. There are other advantages for downsized living spaces.

For the eco-conscious, a large home is not their American dream. They want to leave a smaller environmental "footprint" by using less water and energy than a large home requires. They may choose to walk or ride a bike to work. The suburbs where the reasonably priced houses are may be a long commute to urban work centers. Besides a shorter commute, the culture and entertainment of a downtown lifestyle have their allure. Downsizing Baby Boomers are interested in this kind of lifestyle and so are young, well-educated Millennials and Generation Xers. Some of them enjoy urban living, even though they may be living in a cramped space and paying high prices for groceries and other services. The gratification is immediate, rather than saving up to buy a home.

This lifestyle may need to change when Millennials decide settle to down and start a family, because raising children in the city can be difficult. If you are younger, make a good salary, and are enjoying renting a perhaps a luxury apartment, be aware that your desires could change radically if serious romance and a baby were to enter your life.

Become a skillful tenant

When you choose a place to rent, consider all the aspects that we mentioned in Chapter Two, as if you are going to actually buy the property. This will be your residence, your living quarters, whether or not you own it.

There are ways to save on your rent. One way is to determine if you have some "wiggle room" to haggle or negotiate over the price of your rent. If there are a lot of rental homes to choose from in your area, that is good news for you. Some cities overbuilt new apartment buildings or converted new condo projects into rentals. This means it is "a renters' market" and you can negotiate for better terms. Don't be shy about asking for decreased rent, free months of rent, and perks such as local gym membership. If you know you will be renewing your lease, offer to do it early in exchange for better terms. Also look for signs that your landlord is struggling and may be willing to negotiate. If you notice that there are a lot of vacancies and reduced maintenance, you could be in a position to play hardball. Explain the reasons you need to have your rent reduced, such as you have been laid off, had your work hours reduced, had to take time off for a sick relative or illness, etc. Fear of losing a good tenant is often enough to make landlords reconsider their rent.

Don't get scammed while renting. Don't fall for fake offers such as an email that promises if you send money, you will receive the keys to an apartment. Make sure that the place you are renting actually belongs to the person to whom you are paying rent. Ask for identification and driver's licenses and look at their website. A search on the county recorders or assessor's records will tell you if there is a notice of default or liens against the property that you are renting. This would indicate that your landlord is in financial trouble. If you use a property manager, check out the property manager yourself. For more research, go to www.CheckYourLandlord.com.

Remember to look at all your options

Whether you rent or buy, it makes sense to have a residence that is large enough to have someone live with you. They can be just a tenant, or they could be a friend or family member who could also help you. The help can be mutual. You could keep an eye on an aging parent while they help you keep an eye on your kids, for example. Quite often we come across individuals who have rather modest incomes (most frequently single mothers, in some cases it may be single fathers) who are struggling to get by because housing is taking fifty to sixty percent of their take-home pay. Sharing a residence whether it is in a home or an apartment either by renting, renting a room or renting out a room versus owning a house can make a dramatic difference in one's personal cash flow and progress to financial independence.

You have options you hadn't considered before to save money with your home. Become a do-it-yourselfer. For example, if you have a gardener, mow the lawn yourself. The same goes for housecleaning, painting and minor repairs.

How often do you use your living room or your dining room? A seldom-used area could be repurposed as the play room for the kids or as your office and free up a bedroom for a roommate.

For example, depending on where you live, a one-bedroom apartment may be eight hundred dollars a month and an equivalent two bedroom apartment only twelve hundred. By sharing a larger space with a roommate, you each save two hundred dollars after tax income. This is equivalent to earning an additional three to four hundred dollars per month depending on your tax bracket. There are also substantial savings on sharing utilities and housekeeping supplies.

You can find a list of home-sharing programs at the National Shared Housing Resource Center www.NationalSharedHousing.org. They screen tenants for compatibility and often help negotiate the rental agreements. Churches and civic organizations and community groups also have access to renters' boards and renters' postings and can help you find a roommate.

One secretary told Sam recently that she could live in a much better neighborhood for herself and her child by sharing an apartment, rather than carrying the entire lease on her own. She always wanted to "move up" and she could do so within her income, thus providing a better school and environment for her child.

Housing decisions for seniors

Sometimes maintaining a home is too much of a burden and it is time for a retirement home. Signs that it is time for this change are depression, lack of interest, lateness in paying bills, forgetting names, neglecting to turn off appliances, getting lost, missing doctors' appointments, etc. If this describes your aging loved one, you are stepping into the caregiver role and need to prepare for the best way to manage this transition financially as well as emotionally.

You or your aging loved ones may prefer to "age in place," which means to live at home for the rest of their lives. Depending on the cost of home nurse care and other services in your area, you may save a considerable amount of money. Do your research online and on the phone about adult care facilities, safety evaluations and assistive technology, and also services to relieve caregivers. Here are some resources: The Program of All-Inclusive Care for the Elderly (PACE), which is free for those who qualify for Medicaid Service programs such as Senior Corps which sends volunteers to offer companionship. In some area non-profit support networks called Villages www.vtvnetwork.org volunteers offer tasks such as plumbing and nursing care. Caregiver search and services are listed at www.genworth.com/caregiving and www.aginglifecare.org.

Housing options for seniors

One option is group living among elderly people who will share a large home together with others they know, rather than pay for a traditional nursing home. They can share skills and resources. One resident may be strong enough to handle the housekeeping and laundry, another one may like to cook dinner for the whole group nightly, another may have a car and like to do the grocery shopping, while another less healthy resident may have more financial resources to contribute.

If you need to be in a residential facility, do your research online and on the phone. Check with your local Area Agency on Aging (AAA) www.n4a.org and National Association for Home Care & Hospice www.nahc.org Medicare www.medicare.gov, Leading Age www.leadingage.org. When you find a location you like, negotiate for as many concessions and services as you can. Up for discussion are monthly fees, amenities, and the size of the deposit. Make sure that the facility is on solid financial footing by looking at the audited financial statement and ask about bond financing and whether it is meeting its terms.

Many active seniors are selling their homes and taking to the open road, permanently. They are putting their things into storage and touring around the country in their recreational vehicles, trailers, or vans. They are following the good weather around the seasons, seeing the tourists' sites, and making lifelong friends from around the country at various national and local campers groups. For income, they are taking seasonal jobs at national parks, giving tours as docents, doing grounds and train maintenance, cooking and cleaning at lodges during the high season and repairs and renovations during the off-season.

Save on seniors living with you

Guest houses, "granny flats" or "mother-in-law" studios are options for senior relatives that may need to move in with you. Some homes have such self-sufficient spaces as a free-standing building adjacent to the garage, sometimes called a "casita." A separate entrance provides for privacy of coming and going, and minimal distraction and invasion of privacy of the main house. Also, garages and pool houses can be converted.

Inside the house, basements and attics can be converted. Be sure to think about these spaces for long-term use and consider issues such as stairs, wheelchair ramp access, wider doorways, removing thresholds, installing grab bars in the shower and bathtub, nonslip flooring. In some cases, the roles may be flipped and an adult child may move in with an aging parent to serve as a part-time caregiver.

Whether your senior is living at home, your home, a residential facility, or an RV, they need to have added measures for safety... This is worth the time and money because it will forestall the cost of more assistance or a new living situation. Hire an occupational therapist to recommend installing safety features such as grab bars in the bath and shower. They can also do training on balance and strength skills, www.simplyhome-cmi.com offers monitoring equipment. You can find geriatric-care managers who can help with all aspects of caring for older adults at www.CareManager.org.

Whether you buy or rent, have a roommate or live alone, analyze all the ways you can save money on your biggest monthly investment—your home.

Illustration by Ros Webb

"Kids, we finally figured out how to save for your college education. We signed up with Airbnb. You just need to sleep over at your friends' house five nights per month."

Chapter 3

MANAGING YOUR DEBT AND BUDGETING

"The art of living easily as to money is to pitch your scale of living one degree below your means."

—Sir Richard Taylor

YOUR FINANCIAL STYLE and your spending rate is one of the most critical drivers in the success of your financial plan. A spending rate also is called a "burn rate"—how fast do you burn through your money? Ask the lifestyle vs. legacy question: Which Is more important: to spend or to invest and have financial freedom later? Saving gives you options.

Everyone has their own financial style. In couple relationships, there are four types: driver, passenger, equal collaborators, and divide and conquer. In the driver model, one person dominates while the other person is the innocent bystander passenger. The driver takes the bulk of the responsibility and the passenger abdicates most responsibility. This can be a problem when the passenger has to take the wheel when one partner is no longer the driver, due to the d's such as divorce, disability, disease, death, default, downsizing at the office, etc.

The same applies to unmarried couples living together. But they have additional complications. Consider buying big ticket items such as cars, electronics, and retirement plans separately. In the event of a break up, joint loans and things purchased jointly are complicated. If you buy a home, have it held in joint tenancy with rights of survivorship. Unlike married couples, the courts won't assume you have equal ownership. This will help ensure that you each would own a share equally in the event of a breakup. Also, one of you won't be literally left out in the cold if the other one becomes deceased.

Determine your decision style with your partner

There are two methods to make budget decisions with a partner. One way is to be "equal collaborators." The other way is to "divide and conquer."

With "equal collaborators" method, each partner works side by side in making all key decisions and performing the necessary budget tasks. With the "divide and conquer" method, each partner selects the tasks at which they are most proficient, and takes responsibility for those portions. One of you may be better at managing the household budget, the other may be better at handling investments and savings.

You must communicate often to keep each other informed for it to be a mutual arrangement. Awareness of what each side is doing is an absolute requirement. In a recent study, "divide and conquer" couples stood out as the "super savers." They also reported higher enjoyment of retirement. and increased their capacity to deal with and plan the volume, velocity, and complexity of financial decisions.

Build in treats

Just make sure that the treat is healthy and affordable! If you have a family, give each of your family members a small indulgence every pay period. No treats leads to resentment and "falling off the wagon" of your budget. Just as it is hard to stay on a diet of celery-only for very long, it's hard to stay on a no-treat budget very long. Be realistic about the fact that you need something to look forward to. Everyone's treat budget is different, depending on your income. For some, a treat is a dinner out or a professional massage. For others, it could be a trip to a dollar store and buy $5 worth of "want not need" items. If you reward yourself, you will feel better. The longer you stay on budget, the stronger the good habit becomes.

Try compromising your debt

Your debt is out of control if careful budgeting cannot eliminate it within three to five years. Look at everything including the sale of assets which you don't need, earning extra income, and cutting way back on your expenditures and lending yourself only the most basic need will not be enough.

If these don't solve the problem, you need to compromise your debt. A debt compromise is where the lender agrees to release you from all or a portion of your debt in exchange for putting you on a payment schedule or allowing you to pay a one-time payment. This would be a one-time payment of a discounted amount of debt which you are able to secure by borrowing from friends or relatives or selling an asset.

This may have a negative impact on your credit score and interfere with your ability to borrow in the future or increase your cost of credit in the future. The offering of a compromise has to be carefully considered. This action should only be taken if you're going to clear out all debt that would interfere with you being able to get a fresh start on your way to financial independence.

Do not over-promise what you can do to get out of debt. Be realistic in your assessment of how much of the debt you can discharge within a reasonable period of time. If you are successful in negotiating a compromise and something comes up and interferes with your ability to perform contacts your creditor immediately and explains the circumstances.

The worst thing you can do is to ignore debt. This angers creditors and makes it difficult to compromise or get some postponement in the event that you're not able due to meet your obligations under the compromise. Ignoring debt will make the creditor take a harder position on waving or forgiving penalties and interest charges.

Tell the creditor that when your only alternative is bankruptcy, they possibly will receive nothing. Most creditors would prefer to receive something rather nothing and will be willing to work out a reasonable compromise.

It is extremely important if you are going to compromise that you have something in writing from the creditor that if you meet the obligation the debt will be discharged. The creditor will insist that if the compromise is not met the original amount of the debt will be reinstated less any payments you've made.

Illustration by Ros Webb

Steward: "We have some deluxe suites that are three
times larger, but they are $800 per night."
Couple: "The boat just left the dock.
… We will take one of them for $400."

Chapter 4

MANAGING FINDING NEW MONEY

"There are but two ways of paying debt: increase of industry in raising income, increase of thrift in laying out."
—Thomas Carlyle

IT TAKES LESS TIME and energy to save money than it does to make money. Nevertheless, consider ways to make extra money. This is money that you will save, not spend.

Start your own business

If you are employed, does your employment agreement allow moonlighting, or working outside of your company? Explore working overtime and working extra hours from home. Analyze if you can be productive on your own time.

Propose a trial period with specific required outcomes. Explain all the details, the hours you will be available, and how you can be reached. Plan for your home office space and equipment requirements. An added benefit is the possibility of deducting some of your expenses from your taxes. Seek the advice of a CPA or tax preparer.

If you are retired, you have flexibility with your time. If you like variety and travel, volunteering out in nature, and a simplified life, you could try to find work in the great outdoors. A growing army of about 80,000 retirees work and volunteer at cash-strapped state and federal parks, campgrounds, and wildlife sanctuaries, usually in exchange for camping space. This much-needed army of work-campers lead nature walks or staff visitor centers part-time at a numerous locations. The number of campsites set aside for volunteers has increased twentyfold in the last decade. Contact the National Association of RV Parks & Campgrounds at www.arvc.org.

Find hidden money

Here are some money-making ideas: Put your family members to work. Teens can mow lawns, wash cars, babysit, and work at a fast-food restaurant or movie theater. You can look for focus group companies that will pay you to participate in focus groups. You can find out if money is owed to you by searching online at www.MissingMoney.com, operated by the National Association of Unclaimed Property Administrators. You can dig out those old savings bonds. See if they have matured. Gather your receipts for reimbursements you are owed for money you have already spent, from an employer for company travel expenses.

You can sell old electronics at www.gazelle.com, www. SellCell.com, www.ecyclegroup.com, www.CellForCash.com, www.ibuyphones.com, www.SimplySellular.com, www.SellMy-OldCellphone.com, www.CashOldPhone.com. Find an alternative to your expensive gym membership, such as hiking, biking, and renting workout videos. Collect all those unused gift cards that you received for your birthday and holidays. Make sure that they haven't expired yet. Some experts estimate that the average family has $300 in unspent plastic cash. Most cards can be redeemed online, if that is more convenient for you. If you do not actually need the card, resell it for cash and save the cash. The gift card resale market is thriving online.

You can swap or sell your cards online at www.CardHub. com, www.PlasticJungle.com, www.CardPool.com, www.Gift-Cards.com, www.GiftCardBin.com, and www.SwapAGift.com.

The amount you make will depend on the popularity of the merchant and the amount on the card. If you have already used some of the balance on the card, you can learn the amount remaining by calling the toll-free phone number on the back of the card. Before you send it in, check the buyer's reputation with the Better business Bureau and online reviews. Photocopy your card and keep documentation.

You can search for grants that you may qualify for. Go to www.grants.gov for federal agencies grants and user guide, foundations and private sources that provide funds, such as www.FoundationCenter.org, www.foundations.org, www. GrantSolutions.gov, www.FundsNetServices.com, www.usa. gov, and www.sba.gov.

Return or sell stuff you no longer want or need and you still have the receipts for. You may be one of those people who have clothes in your closet that still have the tags attached. Consignment stores are a great place to get rid of extra or no-longer-needed clothes, furniture, and home accessories.

Clear out the clutter

You have too much stuff in your house. Almost everyone does. You can gain dominion over it with a step-by-step process. Sit quietly and list every category of clutter and its location. Then go room by room, closet and take inventory. Rank the clutter hotspots in order of difficulty, easiest at the top of the list. You may feel overwhelmed with the seeming enormity of your task list that you wish it would disappear. No one is asking you to get rid of everything. You do not want to call the haul-away folks yet. There may be some buried treasure in the piles. Your task is to find it.

If collecting clothes is your weakness, find a good friend who will tell you ruthlessly which items are really "you." Organize your closet by category or by color so you can find things easily. Think like Sarah Jessica Parker, trend-setter television personality and executive producer. A few years ago, she declared her new resolution is to "buy less. Am I really going to wear that pair of shoes? Am I really going to carry that bag?"

First you have to figure out what you can give away. This can be emotionally wrenching, especially if you must sift through a relative's stash. Go easy with yourself. Take it in just 20-minute sessions at a time. Start sequestering the stuff you can live without. Put it in a special place, a corner, a room, the garage. Pick up each item in that clutter hotspot and ask yourself, "If I have not used this in a year, why not? Why am I hanging on to it?" If is just sitting there taking up room and not contributing to your life, it is time to give it a new home, and give yourself new space. Clean out all the storage corners of your home.

If the task is overwhelming, you can hire a professional home organizer. Search online and on www.AngiesList.com. To save money, perhaps you can swap services with the organizer, or offer a percentage of the proceeds of your yard sale. With or without help, accumulate all the many things you can live, without, dust them off, clean them up, and put them into the proper piles.

When you start to see tidiness and order in various corners of your life, you will feel strangely, delightfully energized. When you do not know what to do with something, try visualizing someone else enjoying it. You can gather things to give to friends or a charity. Then tackle another 20-minute session. Rinse and repeat. Go through each pile, closet, and corner of your life, re-sorting everything in one of four piles: the throw away pile, the donating-to-charity pile, the give-to-friends pile, and the resale pile. Next, drag the throw-away pile to the trash. When your resale pile is complete, re-sort that into piles for garage selling and thrift/consignment store selling.

What to do with your stuff

If you are merging households, you may have lots of excess furniture. A good place for it is consignment stores. When Heidi remarried, she enjoyed getting the checks from the local hospital charity consignment store, as they gradually sold each of her furniture pieces. Consignment stores are also a good place for nice, gently used clothing, shoes, and jewelry. The store takes a large percentage, but you do none of the work. They will keep your goods for about three months. If they haven't sold it by that time, they will call you to come and pick up your things. Then you can sell it yourself, give it away, or store it. Remember, "Don't hang on too tight, or you might get rope burn."

The self-storage industry has boomed in recent years. Apparently, Americans need more space to put their stuff. It's not because their homes have gotten smaller. In 1970, the average American home was 1,400 square feet. It is now 2,300 square feet, even though the average size of our households has shrunk from 3.1 to 2.5 people per households. We say there is a high price of acquiring and hanging onto too much stuff—and hidden treasure in divesting yourself of it.

Do you wish you had more storage space in your home? That's a bad sign. The storage industry is built on people not making an effort to deal with their stuff. Instead of paying a storage company at least $100 a month to store your stuff, lighten up and get rid of it! We know friends who pay $200 per month for years to store their furniture. Over time, they could replace the old furniture with new furniture for a fraction of what they spent to store it.

Consider other ways to sell

With over 86 million active users, eBay moved more than $48 billion worth of goods in 2009 alone. Other popular online marketplaces are www.eBid.com, www.bidville.com, www.delcampe.com, www.OverstockAuctions.com, www.ubid.com, www.tanzbar.com, www.craigslist.com, and www.BackPage.com.

You can also sell person-to-person online through posting your ad in www.craigslist.com and some newspaper websites and print newspapers. Give only your email address, perhaps one that you use only for selling purposes. Negotiate via email. When you finally meet the prospective buyer or seller, meet in a public place and bring a friend.

If you go with eBay, train yourself with the help, learning center, and getting-started sections of the site. Get an idea of competitive pricing by looking at how others have priced similar items. Take a well-lit, professional-looking photo of your item with a neutral cloth backdrop.

Since online customers will not be able to examine the item until they have purchased it, be honest about any defects. Include measurements, and comments about the condition, shipping cost, maker, and history. If it is a collectible, examine it closely for more clues. Find out everything you can about it by researching online. Then tell its story. Tell about the good, the bad, and the ugly. Every detail counts. Take lots of pictures to show everything about the item. Take pictures that are clear and easy to see. Do not photograph the clothes on a person, as this is distracting.

Learn the eBay tricks

Err on the side of over-information. You don't want angry buyers demanding their money back and bad-mouthing you on the site because they were under-informed when they bought your item. Answer any inquiries about your items promptly and courteously. Mail your item promptly and with care. Buyers and sellers will comment on your honesty. Negative online reviews are a curse that could ruin your reputation as a seller, so go out of your way to develop a good reputation that will expand your customer base. Use a PayPal account www.PayPal.com for your customers to pay you with. Avoid wire transfers, a common vehicle for scammers.

Price your items carefully. Research what the online competition is charging. You will have hidden expenses, such as listing and commission fees. You can calculate your fees at www.ebcalc.com. www.Auctionbyte, a publication about online auctioning, has a chart of seller fees. You may have to pay for packing and shipping, so find out what that costs first, too. EBay has a shipping center with more information. If you have a collection of designer handbags, check out www.avelle. com (formerly www.BagBorrowOrSteal.com) about renting your bags.

If you want start small, auction off something you don't care much about. Or buy one small item and see how it works. You also can hire a pro to walk you through the process. "Trading assistants" can help with buying, selling, and coaching. You can find these online auction professionals at eBay's trading assistant directory, www.877isoldit.com and www. AuctionItToday.com, or do a Google search. Note that they take a hefty commission.

Illustration by Ros Webb

Girls: "Grandpa, what are you going to do with all your money?"
Grandpa: "Don't worry about it, Girls. I am taking it with me."

Chapter 5

MANAGING YOUR LOVED ONES

*"Be diligent to know the state of your flocks,
and attend to your herds; for riches are not forever,
nor does a crown endure to all generations."*
—Proverbs 27:23

EVERY COUPLE NEEDS to be upfront with each other about their finances, whether you are married, living together, or just roommates. You will be making money decisions with your partner and you need to do it honestly so you can make the best choices.

Kids have no clue

As any parent knows, children are not born with an understanding of money. As the saying goes, "Offer a toddler an ice cream cone or a check for one million dollars, and he will choose the ice cream cone!" Children learn about money very quickly by watching everyone around them. If the parents overspend, the kids will learn to overspend, too. Be a good role model. We advocate a small allowance for children who are old enough to buy something at the store. If they want a treat, they can learn to earn and save their money and buy it for themselves. This fosters independence and responsibility, plus learning the value of saving money.

It was once said, "The easiest way for your children to learn about money is for you not to have any." Young children should not be taught that Mommy and Daddy are able to buy them anything that they could want. When they are young, they want inexpensive things. When they grow older, that changes, and rapidly. Parents with high incomes have a challenge in teaching their children the value of money. They can't tell their kids that they need to economize and cut back because they don't have the money to buy them whatever they want. Therefore, their children are likely to adopt a sense of entitlement and argue that they shouldn't have to get a job or live within a budget.

Give your teen the most valuable gift

If you have children, eventually they will grow up to be teenagers. Use your teenage children's own motivation to be independent. Teach them basic life skills, such as how to change the sheets on their beds, cook, and use the washer and dryer. They should contribute to the daily chores of running the family household such as washing dishes, taking out the trash and lawn care. Their allowance can be increased if the chores are increased. This helps them understand the concept of working for money.

One of the best gifts you can give your teen is help finding their first job. This first job will let them see what basic employment is all about. How they need to compete for a job, earn their boss' respect, be on time, and follow instructions. Their first paycheck is a teachable moment about how to manage money. This moment happens after they see the money that is left after taxes are deducted. When you have "the tax talk," explain gross versus net and income taxes versus FICA taxes (which they won't get back, at least not for a long time). Motivate them to keep their job by helping them choose a "stretch goal," something they want to buy that they can't afford yet.

Some parents are embarrassed to ask the kids to contribute the family income, because the family is invested in appearing affluent when they are actually living beyond their means. For example: Sam knows someone who is on a limited income. His daughter wanted a car, and he bought her an expensive sports car by withdrawing funds from his retirement fund. She did not contribute anything to its purchase. On the other side of the spectrum, Sam knows a young man who parents were very wealthy and bought him an economy car. He is still driving it five years later. The son also contributed to buying it by working as a grocery boy.

At your local bank branch help your teen open up a savings account. Encourage them to commit to deposit a regular amount of each paycheck into the account. When they learn to use their bank, introduce them to the staff, so they will feel comfortable coming in and asking questions. They need to realize the high cost of fees, such as ATM fees and overdraft fees if they overdraw their account. When Heidi took her sons into the bank to open their first checking account, the teller recommended an account that required periodic, mandatory withdrawals into a savings account. If a child is not accustomed yet to balancing their checkbook, they could become overdrawn easily with this kind of account.

Help your adult children wisely

Some college graduates without a positive credit history will have a hard time qualifying for a car loan, renting an apartment, or getting a credit card without their parents' help. Their parents could add them to their credit card as an authorized user. If the grad misuses the card, the parent can remove them as a user. But the parent is still responsible for the balance and any missteps will hurt the parents' rating too. By the same token, if the parent is late on payments, the grad's credit history will be hurt, too. If they co-sign for the account, parents and grads have equal control of the account, which means the parent cannot close the account without the grad's consent.

If your adult children or relatives need to live with you, ask them to donate to household expenses in cash in the amount that would be equal to a rental fee. Save the cash and decide later if you want to give them back some or all of the money.

Use peer pressure

You may need to convince a loved one to assist you in your savings goals or save for themselves. It is not enough to just point out how they will gain by saving. Let them know how it will make you happier and how you can do things with the savings, together. Many people act on something if they hear that by doing so, they will help others. Another technique is to refer, in social conversation, to how others they like are either gaining through savings plans and those they dislike destroying their financial independence. By referring to how much friends are saving, and what they are gaining, you may find that the person you are talking to will tend to follow suit, since we all tend to want to behave similarly to our friends.

Don't let peer pressure be used against you. If you are asked to give a loan to a family member, get a written contract unless you want to give the money as a gift. Lending money to a friend or relative usually creates resentment. Remember that loaning money can cause hard feelings. As Johann Lavater said, "Never say you know a man until you have divided an inheritance with him."

Bring a pet into your life wisely

Concern about animals, both wild and tame has been a growing trend for many years. We believe in pet ownership as long as it is done responsibly. Pets can add greatly to your quality of life, if it is the right pet at the right time. Pet preoccupation and obsession is a fun pastime and topic of conversation. Pet ownership can become an emotional issue, so before you allow yourself to fall into puppy love, know what you are signing up for. Once you take your precious cargo home, it is difficult to turn back the clock. Speaking of the clock, how much can you expect to spend over the lifetime of a cat or dog? You could easily spend more than $10,000. This tally does not count veterinarian bills. Nor does it count the cost of purchasing your pet or the cost of any modifications you might want to make to your home such as dog door, gates, or repairs to furniture.

There is no need to purchase a pet, when you can visit animal shelters. In this economy, humane societies, county animal care services, and shelters are filled with abandoned animals. If you love animals, why not take care of the animals that are abandoned first?

Many shelters offer incentives, such as discounted spaying and neutering. If you are going to pay for a pet, you should pay for it in cash. Go into debt only for the unavoidable necessities of life. When choosing a pet, consider that cats are more independent and generally need fewer vet visits and trips to the groomer. Also consider the breed, for example, Great Dane dogs are more expensive to care for and feed than an average sized dog. Some dogs have more inbred, heredity ailments than others.

Save money on your pet

If you have a pet, do not buy expensive, organic products. Your pet will stay healthier and cost you less in food and vet bills if you follow this simple advice: carefully measure out food and keep treats to a minimum. You can get good pet food for your pet at discount stores. Look for manufacturer coupons. Buy large quantities at a volume discount at www. DrsFosterSmith.com. Super Wal-Mart's www.walmart.com meat department can sell you beef tongue, tripe, and other organ meats that dogs enjoy.

Learn to bathe your pet and trim their nails yourself. Some animal shelters use dishwashing soap instead of expensive pet shampoos. Maybe you can find a groomer-in-training at a local dog grooming school. Generally veterinarians recommend to not feed "people food" to your pet. It can cause them to become overweight and even develop illnesses such as diabetes. For fun toys, do not spend a fortune. Some cats enjoy chasing yarn or ping-pong balls and dogs love balled-up old socks with a bell inside.

Dogs need heartworm medication to keep them from dying due to this deadly parasite. The medications should be prescribed by the vet, but you can search online for discounts and shop at discount stores such as Wal-Mart.

Avoid overpriced veterinarians. We have even seen clinics that advertise "holistic pet care." Spaying and neutering can cost hundreds of collars at a private vet, but less than a hundred dollars at the local Humane Society. If your pet is ill, find a vet that will explain all your options, not just the most expensive one! Find a veterinarian who is willing to work with your budget.

Look for vet specials and low-cost clinics. If your pet needs tests or surgery, weigh the costs, benefits, and the risks. Ask your vet probing questions such as why is this test, procedure, or surgery necessary? Will the vet be able to prolong your pet's life for only a few more months? Is your pet suffering and will the surgery prolong your pet's suffering? What will the total surgery and after-care cost? What are potential complications and what might they cost? Get a full itemization from your vet before you decide. If you decide to go ahead with surgery, work out a payment plan with your vet.

If you decide against surgery, talk with your vet about alternatives. Perhaps there are less invasive procedures and treatments that could make your pet more comfortable and increase your pet's quality of life. Pet veterinarian insurance is available, but please make sure that your own health insurance is the best it can be first.

Pets can be costly. American's spent more than $10 billion on veterinary care last year. That's more than 80% higher than ten years earlier. As much as you love your pet, try to keep a muzzle on the costs. If your pet becomes too expensive, consider offering it to another loving home.

Illustration by Ros Webb

It's all about the labels.

Chapter 6

MANAGING YOUR
PROFESSIONAL SERVICES

"Creditors have better memories than debtors."
—Benjamin Franklin

A SIDE FROM YOUR HOUSE and your car, one of the largest costs that will add up over a lifetime are professional services, from credit card interest, taxes, fees, insurance, lawyers, dentist, and doctors bill, among other professional services. Here is how to manage them all.

Watch out for banking fees

The new culprit is rising fees, which unlike taxes, do not require legislative approval to be imposed. Fees are on the rise. They are getting hard to ignore. As a billboard advertising a financial institution once read, "Money doesn't grow on fees." Fees keep coming because they are tucked away, they are (usually) small amounts, and they are a hassle to resist. Watch for "fee creep" and object to it. Ask for fee reduction, or elimination. If you do not resist, fee creep will grow like a weed.

Banks and financial institutions add fees and note them in the tiny print of the contract that no one reads. When you open a checking account, find out about the account overdraft fees. When you get a debit card, find out if you can be charged an overdraft fee without warning. Ask your bank to deny any purchase or ATM withdrawal beyond the value of your account balance. Sometimes overdrafts are unavoidable. Banks are quick to process checks but can be slow in making deposits. That lag time can be your demise. Know what the hold will be on your deposits.

Expect a delay when you deposit money at an ATM that is not at your bank. Credit cards are charging annual fees more often, so be sure to consider the cost of the fee versus the benefit of accepting the card. Avoid late payment fees by paying early. Ask your credit card company to deny any purchase beyond your credit limit.

As we know, banks may be eager to take money but not always as eager to give it. As Bob Hope once famously jokes, "A bank is a place that will lend you money if you can prove that you don't need it."

Watch out for the downside of online banking

An automatic withdrawal system can help you start saving. Set up a separate savings account and have direct deposit from your employer to your new account. Set up automatic transfer of a portion of your paycheck into the savings account. But leave a sufficient cushion and make sure the deposits happen at the right time so you don't have any problems.

Banks want you to bank online because it costs less than paying human bank tellers. Some banks even charge a fee when you speak with a teller, so ask about that, too. Online banking has some advantages. It can help you monitor balances and transfers into your savings account without making a trip to the bank. It also provides convenience if you pay your bills online and need to receive alerts about notifications on withdrawals and overdrafts. Online banking is usually fast and convenient. You can use direct deposit and automatic bill pay to save time and record your transactions.

This is good as long as there are no technical difficulties or human error. Set up everything very carefully with safeguards from technical and human-error snafus. If there is a glitch, it can spin out of control. The errors can take time and money to correct. Identity theft and cyber security breaches are increasingly common. Be alert for fraud sites set up by hackers that look like your bank's site. They are difficult to detect. Even if the log-in boxes on banks' pages are properly secured, the full page itself can be a redirected to a hacker.

Banking on your mobile device is becoming more common, too. To attract new customers, especially younger ones, Banks are creating apps to allow you to do more banking transactions on your smart phone, such a checking balances, transferring funds, depositing checks, and paying bills and even making payments phone to phone.

Don't become overly dependent on online banking. Arrange your banking habits to include face-time at your bank and get to know the managers. You will be able to get favors done more quickly. Your baking relationships may help you get a loan. If you have any needs or problems, you are not just a number. Your banking relationships may help you get a loan.

Know how to handle credit cards

Credit cards are hard to get right. They can create more problems than they solve. They offer some advantages besides instant gratification. For example, careful use of credit cards can help build or rebuild your credit history. They also can assist in disputing a charge. You can withhold payment on faulty merchandise. That is why you need to keep records of each credit card interaction. If there is a problem that can't be solved with the merchant, you can ask the credit card issuer to withhold the charge.

Do you have the discipline to accept credit card offers and not use the cards? If so, you can increase your total available credit. Credit bureaus look at your debt to available credit ratio. This also is called your "credit utilization ratio." It is the amount of money you've borrowed as a percentage of your available credit. To calculate it by comparing the average of amount of credit card debt you have outstanding against your credit limits. Lenders want to see you borrowing only a fraction of the credit available to you, the lower the better. Some say the magic number is to keep it below 35 percent.

A strong positive credit rating will help with getting approved for a rental agreement, a loan on a car or home, and even getting a job. Be aware that employers run credit checks on potential employees. You can improve your score by always paying your bills on time, keeping your credit card balances low, below $1,000.

If you have discipline, you may choose to keep your credit cards active by using them for a small purchase once in awhile. Just be sure you have the money set aside to pay off the purchase right away. If you try this and you find yourself starting to use the cards again without control, stop using them altogether. Getting into credit card debt and addiction again is far more damaging than having an inactive credit card.

Watch out for the downside of credit cards

As we said in our first book, don't pay just the minimum balance on your cards, or you will barely cover the interest and it will take years—and potentially thousands more dollars—to pay off the balance. Credit cards can damage your credit if you have a late payment.

Sometimes it seems like banks are offering too many credit cards. Sometimes it seems like they don't offer enough cards. If you are offered lots of credit cards, beware. Don't use them. If you want more cards to be offered to you, pay off the ones you have. But don't cancel them. If you take advantage of a 0 interest offer, be sure to pay off the entire balance in full very early. Or the new interest rate will shock you. Opening up a new account may also ding your score, but only temporarily, as long as you make payments on time and don't ring up a huge debt. It is better to use the card only when you can do so without incurring a balance. Credit card debt is often your most expensive debt.

Credit cards that give rewards cards actually can be unrewarding. Make sure that the rewards are for products and services you want. Otherwise, what's the point in paying the higher interest rate? If you really need the airline miles, then use the card that gives them to you. But don't get miles for trips that you cannot afford to take! Rewards cards can tempt you to spend more money. They often have an annual fee, so decide if the rewards are really going to be worth it. Instead go for cash rewards, which have more uses.

Another thing that can demolish credit isn't a thing; it's a person—your significant other. Be in agreement about how your joint credit cards will be used. If you have shared debt as most married couples do, and you get divorce, joint credit cards may be your responsibility, too. Consult your attorney and tax preparer or CPA about having those balances transferred to new credit cards in the appropriate person's name.

Know how to obtain credit cards

Find a credit union that offers credit cards and join the credit union with a small savings account before you apply. Many credit unions are open to everyone who lives in the area. Pick a credit union where deposits are insured by the National Credit Union Administration. To find one nearby, search online and click on www.creditunion.coop/cu.com and www.culookup.com.

If you need credit but do not have a credit card, ask your local bank or credit union for a small loan. Offer to maintain a specific balance in the account, which they can take if you don't make your payments. Be certain that your good behavior is reported to the credit bureaus. When applying for credit, take it slow. Don't apply for too many at one time. Watch for hidden rate hikes. Watch for fees for fines for late payments. Late fees represent as much as one-third of the income of some credit-card issuers. Use each card for a small amount periodically and then put the card away. Pay off the entire balance in full every month. Remember, paying interest works against you in the same way that earning interest works for you when you invest.

Know how to control your credit cards

First pay down the credit cards with the highest interest rates, since those are the ones that are costing you the most. If you have a lot of cards with a small balance, pay those off too to gain confidence that you can, in fact, gain mastery over the credit monkey that has been riding on your back.

Make sure to rotate your cards, and use a different one periodically. Some cards are suspended if they are not used enough. Find out the requirements on your card so that it is not suspended due to inactivity. If you want to transfer balances to a card with a lower interest rate, consider both the interest rate and the balance transfer fee, which can be large. Cash advance fees should be noted, too. Read the fine print to find maintenance fees and inactivity fees.

Ideally, you would lock up the cards and let the accounts lapse for lack of use, rather than cancelling, which could hurt your credit score by reducing your available credit overall. Try to get a new card with a lower interest rate before letting the old card lapse. If you want out of a reward card with an annual fee, ask the company to waive the fee or swap for a no-fee card.

Don't cancel your credit cards. Even if the rate is increased or your credit limit is cut, that card is still a useful part of your credit health. Cancelling cards reduces your available credit that might be needed in an emergency. It also deprives you of an account that helped establish your credit history. The length of time you've had a credit account is a major factor in determining your credit score.

Know how to handle credit counseling

A legitimate credit counseling agency can help you prepare a debt management plan to reduce your debt. The company would obtain agreements and concessions from your creditors. Then they would handle your debt payments from a monthly deposit you make. Read your debt settlement agreement carefully before signing. When you sign the agreement, you will be obligated to live within the restrictions, such as you cannot take on additional credit. Be sure you understanding what you are signing. But a DMP is a serious step. Know that negotiating a lower rate is likely to hurt your credit score.

But if your score is already low and you are struggling, it may help you stop the bleeding. You may be in trouble if you can afford to only make minimum payments on your credit cards or you have used a home equity loan to refinance credit card debts and then run up new balances on your cards. You are in danger zone if you have been considering payday loans and title loans against your car.

If you ran into credit problems and are considering credit counseling, watch for scams. If you are worried that you might be headed for foreclosure, don't put your head in the sand. The sooner you ask for help from your mortgage company, the better your chances of minimizing the damage. Pick up the phone while there is still time. Depending on which state you live in, missing three to four mortgage payments can lead to "foreclosure start." Open and respond to all mail from your lender. The first notices you receive will offer how to prevent foreclosure, follow it. Find your loan documents and read them so you know what your rights are.

Every state has different foreclosure laws, so read up on them. Contact a HUD-approved housing counselor. The U.S. Department of Housing and Urban Development (HUD) funds free or very low-cost housing counselors who can help you explore your options and help you with negotiations. Call (800) 569-4287. Above all, avoid foreclosure prevention companies or lose your house to a foreclosure recovery scam

If you hire a credit counselor, look for a credit counseling agency that is a nonprofit, tax-exempt agency that charges you little or nothing. They should be willing to offer you information about its services free of charge. Their employees should not be paid on commission. Look for credit counseling services that are approved by the U.S. Department of Housing and Urban development. The National Foundation for Credit Counseling publishes lists of accredited companies and guidelines for selecting the right credit counselor on www. DebtAdvice.org.

Know how to avoid credit counseling scams

There is a difference between credit counseling services and credit repair services (also known as a debt settlement services). Most of the companies that offer to fix your credit score are scams. Watch for those that have pre-payment requirements. Don't allow a company to suggest that you invent a new credit identity. You would be committing fraud. Check for accreditation with the National Foundation for Credit Counseling www.nfcc.org. Before you sign anything or pay any money, do your due diligence. Do a background check and contact your county or state consumer protection office of the Better Business Bureau.

Signs of a scummy credit counseling operation are: offering to loan you money, offering to sell your name to other lenders, or offering to dispute truthful but negative information on your credit report. They should not charge upfront fees or con you into signing over the deed to your house. They may even offer to create a new identity for you. This is illegal, obviously. If they tell you to stop paying your bills, run the other direction.

Don't use a debt settlement firm which charges a large upfront fee for their services. Avoid agencies that urge you to declare bankruptcy, tell you that your credit score will not be affected, ask for a percentage of any savings, or guarantee that your debts can be eliminated or that you can be protected from lawsuits.

Know how to stand up for your rights

A great way to save money is to be a consumer advocate—advocating for yourself as a consumer. Do not pay upfront before you get services. Reputable companies will not make you pay in full until the service is complete. If you get no help, contact the Better Business Bureau, state or federal agencies that regulate the business, local and state elected officials, the state attorney general, industry trade associations, and finally Small Claims Court. A free guide at www.ConsumerAction.gov will help. The Federal Trade Commission at www.ftc.gov tracks bad companies and how to avoid them. It does not resolve individual consumer complaints, but it does file suit against companies with a pattern of bad practices.

If you need to make a claim against a company, keep your cool. First, decide what you want to have happen. Know the fine print in the contracts and warrantees, especially the refund or cancellation policy. Otherwise, the company will confront you with it. What will make this problem right for you? Contact the seller. Say, "I am very upset because x happened. I need you to correct this situation. To make it right, I need to have y happen." Communicate your position briefly, calmly, and effectively. If you write an email, be brief and accurate. Think "concise and precise." Then start crawling up the hierarchy of management. Keep copies of absolutely everything (receipts, packaging, and emails) and detailed records (time, date, name, phone numbers and what was said). Get in writing whatever they promised to give you. Oral promises are often worthless.

Keep professional fees to a minimum

Our first book has a section on saving money on medical needs. Here are a few more tips: Your doctor can advise you on which websites are legitimate for buying from alternative pharmacies that are lower priced for the same quality. Also tell your doctor that you are open-minded about trying alternatives to pharmaceutical medications, such as natural or "home remedies," which are often less expensive and healthier. When you experience a physical symptom, save money and time by being proactive. Prepare for your doctor's exam by first researching the symptoms on the Internet and writing out a list of questions. Also keep a journal about your condition, which will help your doctor diagnose it more accurately.

Find a good lawyer

Almost everyone will, at least once in their life, need to consult an attorney in connection with wills, taxes, divorces, criminal charges, real estate, lawsuits, etc. Law touches every aspect of our daily life, and thousands of dollars can be saved through good legal advice and planning. The use of lawyers is expensive but in many cases can result in savings far in excess of their cost. The trick in saving on legal fees is in knowing how to efficiently and effectively find the right lawyer at the right price for the right answer.

A good source of lawyer references are your other professional advisors such as your banker, accountant, or insurance advisor. They deal with lawyers daily and will be familiar with many of those in your area and their competence. Relatives who have had experience with lawyers may also be a good source. It is important when you have legal problems to consult a lawyer as early as possible. The longer you delay, the more costly it will become. A half hour to an hour of a lawyer's time before you sign a contract, reviewing the contract, can save you thousands of dollars and hours and hours of time, attempting to get out of a disadvantageous contract.

Many local bar associations have lawyer reference services where the first half hour is complimentary and can refer you to lawyers who specialize in the matter with which you are concerned. In many cases, lawyers who are connected with legal referral services or younger lawyers who are getting started, as well as specialists, will provide the first meeting free of charge to discuss whether or not they will undertake the matter. Good lawyers do turn down business when they feel it is a matter beyond their competence or when there may be a conflict of interest.

Save on attorney fees

To save on attorney's fees, do your own research your legal situation online, at the library, and at the bookstore before you meet with an attorney. Become familiar with some of the legal terms and definitions of your situation. Prepare a detailed list of questions. Most attorneys charge several hundred dollars per hour, and whatever you can do to lighten their load or find answers yourself will obviously result in substantial savings.

Get clear before your first meeting how the attorney charges and what he or she will charge for. Be sure to explain what your resources are up front, so that you don't get involved in a transaction where the legal fees can exceed your resources. Ask for a list of services the attorney is offering and cost estimates. All lawyers are required to provide these, so use that information to decide if your legal costs would be cost effective. Some transactions have a standard fee, such as for incorporating a company or drafting an agreement. If the attorney quotes a number of hours for the project, multiply that by the hourly rate. Allow for the possibility that it may overrun that time. Tell the attorney that you are on a budget and want to put a cap on your expenses.

When you do consult with an attorney after being adequately prepared, be sure to ask what more you can do to keep the cost down. For example, if you're going to need a contract, go to the Internet, and get the form contract. Fill it out in as much detail as you can, as it will guide you in what you'll need to cover in your meeting with the attorney you have selected. Even on transactions involving many thousands of dollars, Sam always uses this approach when he needs to consult with a specialist. He will find a sample contract or template, prepare it as best he can after educating himself on the special nature of the transaction, and then take it to a lawyer who specializes in that transaction for review and comment. This usually ends up in his needing only one hour of the lawyer's time, whereas if you ask the lawyer to prepare the contract, it could be as many as three to ten hours. It's much less expensive to have a lawyer review a document than to prepare a document.

Before you meet with a lawyer, ask his assistant what documents you should bring with you, such as tax returns, deeds, contracts, invoices, etc. Bring all correspondence and material you have with you that relate to the transaction or matter on the first visit. Sometimes it will help to write out a narrative of what you believe the issue is and what defenses or claims you may have. This will help you and the lawyer focus on the problem. Whatever you present to your lawyer is usually protected by the "attorney-client privilege" which simply means that anything that you disclose to your lawyer in connection to the matter for which he is representing you, is confidential, although there are some exceptions to this, such as, if you are planning to harm yourself or others. In normal business and domestic matters, the privilege will apply.

While social conversation is a way of getting acquainted and comfortable with each other, try to limit it, since if it is done in connection with a legal consultation, you may be charged for it. Sam likes to tell the story of the doctor who, at a party, consulted his lawyer friend with the following question, "I've been asked by one of my patients here, at the party, what to do for a pain they have. I knew immediately what to prescribe and told him what he needed. Should I charge him?"

The lawyer replied, "Yes, charge him whatever you would normally charge for an office visit." The next day, the doctor got a bill from the lawyer for $100, which read, "For consultation advising you to charge your patient: $100."

Know how to save money when visiting the dentist

"Money is the most envied, but the least enjoyed. Health is the most enjoyed, but the least envied." Such is the wise observation of Charles Caleb Colton. Anyone who has ever had a tooth ache can agree that health includes dental health.

Ask questions when you are at the dental office. Dental professionals love to give oral hygiene instructions and tips on home care. Brush with a manual toothbrush at the office after lunch. Floss your teeth while you watch television before you go to bed. Sonic toothbrushes still don't eliminate the necessity of flossing. The better you are at flossing, the healthier your gums and the easier your visits with the hygienist. If you can't floss, an oral irrigating device (water pick) is a great option.

Ask your dentist for very specific advice based on your dental condition. Make sure that you fully understand any treatment being suggested and all options and potential outcomes. Most offices can show you a picture of the area in question.

Use the dental team as your resource for insurance coverage information, benefits and limitations, but don't be afraid to call your carrier yourself. Discuss the timing and prioritization of any treatment. It may save you money to complete prioritized procedures before they become more complex. It may make sense to spread some treatment out over time for maximum insurance benefit. It may also make sense to get a second opinion; most offices will do consultations at no charge.

Invest wisely

Investing is to buy something that you will hold on to, in hope or expectation that it will grow in value over time. Consuming is the opposite. It is when you buy something that you will use up, and therefore it has declining value once you acquire it. You can invest other resources besides money. Investing can be the expenditure of your time and effort. It can be an exchange of your possessions or your skills and services.

Before you invest in anything, look at what resources you

have to give in exchange. What time, money, effort, goods, and services do you have to offer? We all have resources that can be invested or consumed by others. We all have more resources than we realize.

Whatever you do, don't get fooled into investing in a scam or "fast money." If it looks too good to be true, it probably is. As Proverbs 13:11 says, "Wealth gained hastily will dwindle, but whoever gathers little by little will increase it."

The safest approach is to focus on rental income, not appreciation. As one investor said, "Appreciation is the icing on the cake; cash flow is the meal for me." Flipping is for those who have the financial resources to hold the property for as long as it takes to sell it. Rehabbing can take more time and more money than estimated, and usually does. Allow extra funds for those unplanned delays.

Take a close look at your emotions about your decision. Successful investing is a balance of emotional hopes and rational, unemotional expectations. To speculate on an investment is to invest in something with an unpredictable outcome. Don't speculate with money that you need to save.

Don't become "intaxicated"

There is a joke going around that is the definition of the made-up word, "intaxication." Intaxication is defined as euphoria at getting a refund from the IRS, which lasts until you realize it was your money to start with. So whose money is it, anyway? It is yours until you have to give it away. Remember that you may be giving more of it away than you expected. Much of the money will be given away without even noticing it. For example, sales taxes in many states are going up.

Your net worth is what you own minus what you owe. Add up all your assets (the value of your real estate, your paid-off cars, cash on hand, money in checking and savings accounts, CDs, and insurance plus retirement and investment funds such as stocks, bonds, and mutual funds, the cash value of your life insurance, your vested equity in pension and profit-sharing plans, annuities, and valuables such collectibles, jewelry, equipment, furniture, etc.) Then subtract all of your liabilities (your mortgages, equity lines, student loans, other loans, personal debts such as credit card debt, car loans, car payments, etc.) The balance is your net worth.

Live rich; don't die rich

Samuel Johnson, a wise advisor, is quoted as saying, "It is better to live rich than to die rich." In these days of rising taxes, that has never been more true. It takes more effort to hang onto what you make than ever before. We believe in paying our "fair share" and would never recommend tax evasion. However, too many pay more in taxes than is legally required. They are unaware of how taxes here and there add up. As an IRS auditor is quoted as saying cynically, "The trick is to stop thinking of it as 'your' money."

Sam believes that the largest annual expenditure of the majority of our readers is their federal, state, and local income taxes. Here are some lessons he has learned, in a lifetime of owning and running businesses, to handle taxes. If you are fortunate enough to be in the top income bracket, Sam's advice will be very helpful. If not, you should aspire to be in their ranks. Someday you will be, if you apply the savings techniques in our books! If you have taxable income, what you pay for an item costs more that the list price. That's because you have to pay a tax on the amount you paid in taxes. Please see the chapter on taxes in our first book for a detailed example. State, federal, and other income-related taxes will continue to rise. Therefore, it is crucial to consider all of the opportunities to reduce your taxable income.

Sam's Tax Tips

1) Have a clear understanding of the difference between tax evasion and tax avoidance. Tax evasion is illegal. Tax avoidance is legal. Tax evasion can result in serious financial penalties and possible incarceration. Tax avoidance is paying only what is legally required.

2) An example of legal, ethical, reasonable tax avoidance is taking advantage of all the deductions and credits which the tax laws allow. An example of illegal tax evasion would be failing to report income or taking unqualified and unsubstantiated deductions.

3 If you are concerned that your income taxes are rising, talk with your CPA or tax advisor to review your income and expenditures. Your advisor can offer advice and guidance that can make a significant difference. Good tax advisors are worth the money. Your CPA or tax advisor can explain your legal options, which may affect how your conduct your finances throughout the year.

4) Keep a record of expenditures and receipts to support allowable deductions.

5) Consult your tax advisor about the best way for you to report your expenses. For example, consider the current laws regarding gift taxes. Parents who pay for children's medical, education, and certain other specified expenditures by paying the provider directly may in some cases not incur a gift tax. However, gift tax exemptions my not qualify by giving the money to the child and having the child pay the expenditures. This may apply to children giving to parents as well.

6) While there are many elements to consider with regard to real property taxes, there is a wide variance on the values of one's home depending on where it is located, when it was purchased, and how local property tax rates are determined.

7) Your legal residence, for tax purposes will have a major impact on your state tax rate. You also have to consider whether or not your county, municipal or special district taxes affect your income. State income tax can range from 0 to 10% of taxable income. States with no income tax include Nevada, Florida, Alaska, South Dakota, Texas, and Washington, at the time of the preparation of this book.

8) There is a marriage penalty. That means that a family with two income earners may have a lesser federal income tax if they file separately.

9) Be charitable, but in a way that helps you keep more money that you can then give away. Consider how your charitable contributions are made. This may determine the extent of their deductibility and best way to give to them. For example, donating appreciated property under the right circumstances will result in a deduction for the full amount of the property. To sell the property first while still owned may result in taxable gain leaving less net proceeds to donate and available for deductibility.

10) If you have substantial assets that will gain interest in the future, talk to your tax advisor first. There are advantages of various techniques for providing for a future interest in assets to a qualified charity. This could result in current deductions which may improve your current cash flow with no change in your circumstances. The interest would pass to the charity some time in the future.

PART II:

Manage Your Money Mindset

Illustration by Ros Webb

*"Hi Honey! We can't go out for dinner tonight!
I spent all of our money saving it—at the sale!"*

<u>Chapter 7</u>

MONEY MIND SET: TIME IS MONEY

*"It requires a great deal of boldness and a great deal of
caution to make a great fortune, and when you have it,
it requires ten times as much wit to keep it."*

—Ralph Waldo Emerson

MONEY IS VALUABLE, but time is more valuable.
Without time, it doesn't matter how much money
you have. Many waste time more flagrantly than they
waste money, but you should value time even more. Your
most important expenditure is your time. How you spend
time has a major effect on what you will be able to save and
whether you reach your goals. Budgeting time is essential for
personal, professional, and financial success.

People who save money know how to save time. When you
spend time on your education, acquisition of skills, planning
your financial future, improving your health, and strengthening
your significant relationships, your life becomes fuller and
richer and your ability to accomplish is enhanced. If you ignore
these, you postpone your success. When you consider a time
commitment, calculate the impact on your money as well.

Time lost is opportunity lost

By making a choice in one direction means that you lost
the opportunity to benefit from a choice in another direction.

The concept of lost opportunity applies to time. For example, Heidi had a friend who was a highly paid software designer who was laid off when the company closed in the recession. She received almost a year of severance pay for her two years of employment. The bad news is that she spent the money on a trip to South America.

When she returned, she realized that getting her next job would require additional training to be competitive. High paying jobs were offered to her but in each case she lost out because she didn't have the qualifications. Looking back, she remembered that her employer had offered to pay for the time and training to obtain these qualifications. But she hadn't spent the time to get them.

Another example is doing good work for no pay. A friend of Heidi loves helping non-profits, a worthy endeavor. Unfortunately, this has caused a stressful situation as she spent more time on her non-profit work than on finding the new job she needs. Remember to balance your professional goals and needs with your desire to contribute. In our first book we suggested that you "Put your own oxygen mask on first." This applies to your time as well as your money. You cannot help others if you yourself need help.

The value of time

If you had more time in your life, you could take on a part-time job or spend more time studying money-saving techniques. Here are ways to look at how time can make a difference and why time matters: A century matters. Ask an historian. A decade matters. Ask a medical school graduate. A year matters. Ask a child waiting to start kindergarten. A quarter matters. Ask a company that missed earnings projections. A month matters. Ask the mother whose baby was born early. A week matters. Ask a student who didn't study enough to pass. A day matters. Ask a candidate awaiting election results. An hour matters. Ask someone sitting in a doctor's lobby. A minute matters. Ask someone who missed their plane. A second matters. Ask a driver who just ran a red light. A millisecond matters. Ask a sprinter who won a silver medal.

Here are time-saving techniques. Today, take the ones that you can implement easily and try them out for a month. After 21 days behavior becomes a habit. These habits will help you make the time to reach your savings goals.

Be effective with your time

Effectiveness is doing the right things. Efficiency is doing things right. When you have a choice, choose effectiveness. It is more important to do the right thing than to do things right. Usually, if the choice is between the Important versus the urgent, take care of the urgent first, if it has to be done. Otherwise, drop it. If it really needs to be done, do it as efficiently as possible. Do not let the urgent distract you from the Important. Never overlook the importance of the Pareto Principle (the 80/20 rule), which states, "80% of results will come from 20% of effort."

Try to prevent urgent crises by being proactive. When a crisis occurs, figure out how to prevent it from recurring. Ask, what is the worst-case scenario? Focus on important, long-term goals. Spend time on planning how to create more time. Write down your personal and professional goals. Share them with stakeholders. Break down your long-term goals into monthly, weekly, and daily tasks. Make specific goals for each of your many roles, such as parent, spouse, significant other, son/daughter, employer/employee, sibling, friend, community member, etc. Make sure you are giving sufficient attention to each of your roles.

Also see: *How to Get Control of Your Time and Your Life* by Allen Laykin, www.TaylorInTime.com and www.DavidCo.com.

You become more effective when you proactively foresee and prevent urgent emergencies and eliminate them as much as possible. Sometimes the urgent will become the important if it is not given immediate attention, such as caring for your health. Effectiveness and efficiency do not always go together. In other words, if you do something fast, it may take more time to go back and clean up the mistake if you had done it slower, but correctly, the first time. Here are phrases to help you. Important versus Urgent: Choose *Important*. Needs versus Wants: Choose *Needs*. Invest versus Speculate: Choose *Invest*. Save versus Spend: Choose *Save*. Simple versus Complex: Choose *Simple*. Listening versus Talking: Choose *Listening*. Analysis versus Anger: Choose *Analysis*. Ask First versus Act First. Choose *Ask First*.

<u>Be effective with other people's time</u>

You need to respect your time as well as other people's time. Coordinating schedules with your friends, family, and colleagues will strengthen your relationship. How you attend a meeting or how you conduct a meeting determines whether it will be time well spent. Distribute an agenda ahead of the meeting, with estimated time for each topic. Announce the meeting will start and end on time ("cell phone time").

Encourage efficiency by trying brief, daily, stand-up meetings, or meetings during lunch or breakfast. Go around the room and have each person give a two-sentence or two-minute update on their goals or progress. Set a timer for each update so they will be succinct.

Talk about target dates of completion of the next action step to achieve your joint goals Everyone should leave the meeting with a specific, individual commitment to a plan of action and a deadline for completion. At the close of the meeting, request feedback on how it could have been improved. Email the meeting notes to everyone who attended and should have attended. At the follow-up meeting, review the plan of action in the notes to make sure everyone is on track.

Be effective and efficient
in communicating with others online

Be effective and efficient in online communication. When a response to an email is appropriate, acknowledge it as soon as you read it, even if only a very brief message, such as thanks, okay, maybe, let me check, or I'll get back to you on that. Give a time when you will respond further. Don't let email monopolize your day. Check your email only at scheduled periods during the day, such as at 10 a.m. and 3 p.m., or between your appointments. Inform the people you work with of your "email checking" times, so they know they have to wait for your response. Online, use good "netiquette:" Do not use all caps (this denotes yelling). Use lots of courtesy, such as "I apologize," "please" and "thank you." Hurt feelings take more time to fix than to be extra courteous.

Make the goal of your email clear. Ask a specific question or request a specific action at the end of each email. Examples are: Is this helpful? Is there anything else you need from me? Would you please share your thoughts on this?

Be efficient on the phone and in person

Phone calls can be a time waster or a time saver. Keep phone calls brief and to the point, but still be courteous. People will be more inclined to take your call and return your call if they know the call will not consume their lunch hour! Always leave a message or a voice message. It is annoying if someone called but did not leave a message.

Voice messages should include a specific request and the best time to return your call. Use phone calls when a back-and-forth conversation would help you make a complicated decision or when you need to strengthen your connection with that person. Use email whenever possible. It is the best way to exchange detailed information, because it is written out and can be read and analyzed and responded to after being properly considered.

Your precious, one-on-one time should be reserved for two kinds of people: people whose company you truly enjoy, and people who need to meet with you to discuss topics that require more direct interaction than a phone call provides. The person who went to the trouble to meet with you deserves more attention than the person trying to email, text, or phone you during the meeting. Give your face-time partner the respect they deserve. Do not offend them by taking phone calls or checking your emails or texts. Give your undivided attention to them.

Be efficient when organizing your day

Be honest about how much time an activity will require. One of the biggest time sappers is travel and commute time. Schedule more time than anticipated for traveling to and from meetings. In your calendar, post the time that you need to leave for a meeting and the time you need to arrive at the meeting. There often will be necessary delays in entering and exiting regular activities (dropping the kids off at practice, ending a business meeting, etc.) Just take a deep breath and be glad that you built in that extra time buffer so you don't have to stress about being late.

Cluster your activities and locations. Group your activities and errands around centralized locations as much as possible. This applies to mundane activities such as choosing a nearby grocery store and major decisions in life such as where you work. If you are choosing a location in which to start your business, find an office that is close to your home and is convenient for clients. It should be close to a good restaurant where you can entertain your clients. If you work out at an athletic club often, choose one that is close to your office or your home.

Be efficient in organizing your life

Have a place for everything and put everything in its place. Looking for misplaced items is a waste of time and money. Designate separate binders and files for each client or project. Toss, file, delegate, or schedule each piece of paper. Tear out pages, don't keep the whole publication. Keep checklists for recurring events such as meetings and trips. Create template form letters and office materials. Cross reference and make duplicates of important information.

Develop routines. Make it a routine to get up, dress up and show up each day. What tasks do you do daily? Put them on autopilot. Make to-do lists, lay out your clothes, and pack your briefcase the night before. You can take advantage of opportunities if you are prepared.

Schedule your days, weeks, months, and years. Daily determine what three big projects must be accomplished for it to be a success. Keep a list of those projects along with the necessary emails and phone calls. First make the calls or tackle the tasks that you are uncomfortable doing, perhaps because of fear of rejection. Allow for new ideas: keep a pad of paper by your bed, in the bathroom, and in the kitchen. Write down ideas as soon as they come to you so you don't have to remember them. Use travel time, commute time, and exercise time for brainstorming or listening to books on tape.

Be respectful of your time

Time used wisely equals money. Ask yourself at least three times a day, "What is the best thing for me to be doing right now?" Put boundaries around your time. When you are asked to do something extra that you cannot do, should not, or do not want to do, learn to say, "I'm sorry, I can't," or "No, that task would be better for someone else to do. If you change your mind later, you can always come back and say, "I am happy to say that I can help out after all." But say "no" to unnecessary jobs and projects that have no real value in your life. Set aside

needed time for necessary projects as an appointment with
yourself that you keep, as if you were meeting with your boss.
If you are procrastinating, ask yourself what are you avoiding
and why?

Illustration by Ros Webb

"Dad, how about we raise my allowance—
to help stimulate the economy!"

Chapter 8

MONEY MIND SET WITH NEGOTIATING AND BARGAINING

"Money was never a big motivation for me, except as a way to keep score. The real excitement is playing the game."

—Donald Trump

EVERYTHING IS NEGOTIABLE these days. The first hurdle is fear of embarrassment. It is all about how you ask. The key is: Don't be afraid to ask. "If you don't ask; you don't get." The worst thing that can happen is you hear the word "no." With practice, it gets easier, and you start to save money and enjoy the process. While men tend to be more comfortable negotiating than women, women are often successful at negotiating a good price, because when they do it, they do it with subtlety and courtesy.

Negotiate better terms

Review your options before you negotiate, and make sure you understand what's included in the price. Know what a fair price is. Bring evidence of competitor's prices. You can bring in a printed advertisement or check the price on your cell phone. For comparing prices, you can use what is called a shopping "bot," such as www.BizRate.com, www.DealTime.com, www.MySimon.com, and www.Shopping.com.

Stores like to keep your business by matching their competitor's prices. If the price is suspiciously low, do some snooping. Has the box already been opened? Is the written material on the box only in a foreign language? For more information on any specific retailer, you can check user reviews on websites such as www.yelp.com, and www.angieslist.com, www.shopping.yahoo.com. Find out where the hidden costs are hiding.

Deals offered over the phone are hard to enforce. Get a line-by-line breakdown in writing of the price before agreeing to anything. Spend the time necessary on the phone. Your time can equal money in your pocket. Remind customer service about your loyalty and on-time payment history. To get a better operator, call back or ask for someone else. Note their name and # and comments. Ask for your complaints to be logged into your file. Call back every quarter to try to sweeten the deal. Reject extra fees and unneeded services BEFORE they get added to your bill.

Know where to pop the "discount?" question

A perfect place to negotiate is where the markup is excessively high. Research the price of other stores first, so you can accurately claim that the item is less expensive elsewhere. You can tell the store manager that you are deciding between making the purchase at their store or the other store. Negotiating is almost expected in the furniture and jewelry business because the prices are commonly increased three or four times the value of the merchandise. For items that require delivery, you can inquire, "That price includes delivery, right?" If you have a truck and you and a friend can deliver the item yourself, let them know you are a motivated buyer. Keep an eye out for extras that the store can throw in to sweeten the deal, such as accessories or warrantees.

Retailers know they shouldn't charge full price for "damaged goods." As we mentioned in our first book, *TheSmartestWay™ to Save—Why You Can't Hang Onto Money and What To*

Do About It, you can negotiate on big ticket items such as appliances, equipment, and computers at big store chains. Watch for display models, merchandise on clearance or suffering minor dings, or things have been collecting dust on the showroom floor. Smaller stores are better for the "can I buy two and get one free?" type of wheeling and dealing. Try non-chain stores where the owner is the key decision maker. Talk to them when the store is not busy. Conduct your discussion away from other shoppers, if possible. The store will not want to advertise that they gave you special treatment. Maybe the store can throw in an additional item free or at a discount. Say, "I have only x amount to spend on this today." If you are buying in bulk, ask for a volume discount. If you have cash, you will have the upper hand so the retailer can avoid credit card fees.

Look for items on close-out or the sale rack. In the supermarket, it's easy to get a discount on perishable food that is about to expire. The secret to negotiating is to be more than willing to walk away from the negotiation. If you do, leave on good terms, so you can try again next time.

Know when to pop the "discount?" question

The best time to ask retailers for a deal is between seasons. That's when the seller is motivated. They need to get rid of last year's model of car before the new year's models roll in. They need to get rid of the lawn furniture at the end of summer and coats at the end of winter.

Inquire if the item you want is going to go on sale anytime soon. If so, could that promotional price be offered to you today? Maybe they can throw in free shipping, delivery, or installation? If you want to buy a large number of items, say, "I'm buying a lot. Would it be possible to get a discount?" If you are told, "Only the manager can give discounts," respond with "That's fine," and wait for the manager.

Know how to negotiate professional fees

You may not have considered negotiating professional services related to your legal, accounting, and medical needs. For example, you should feel free to ask your accountant for a discount if you submit your tax information early.

If you medical plan doesn't cover a procedure, ask your doctor if he or she can compromise on the price. Heidi had to do this recently, when she had a mammogram and her insurance carrier said that she should have waited a full twelve months after her prior one. Heidi argued with the doctor that his office should have cleared the procedure before it was performed. As a result of her insistence, the price was reduced substantially.

Know how to shop at yard sales and garage sales

Yard sales and garage sales are a perfect place to practice your negotiating skills. Show up early to find the best pickings. But to get the best price, don't buy in a hurry. If you can wait, come back at the end of the sale. At the end of the sale is the best time to negotiate because the sellers are trying to get rid of everything. Say, "I'll offer you (name your price) for that item or group of items." Don't quote your price first; ask them what they would be willing to price it at. If you like to shop at yard sales, look for sales in the local newspapers and online at www.craigslist.com and www.recycler.com, map out your route, carry enough cash, but nothing larger than $20 bills. Bring out extension cords and batteries to try out the merchandise. You have a stronger bargaining position if you look like an informed, cautious shopper.

Much of the strategy for shopping at garage sale applies to shopping at flea markets and public sidewalk sales. However, now you won't be on your home turf. Check out the market first and find out the best traffic patterns. More tips on yard sales can be found in our first book.

Know how to return merchandise

Retailers are developing stricter guidelines for returns. Some stores keep track of the total amount of merchandise you return each year. When you receive a gift, don't open the box until you are sure you want to keep the item. CDs and DVDs with broken seals usually can be only exchanged for an identical item. If you give a gift, include a gift receipt, which has all the information except the price. Don't wait too long to return the item. If you return within 15 days you should be safe. Most bricks-and-mortar stores allow returns of online purchases, but shipping costs may be subtracted from your refund.

When returning merchandise, do not take no for an answer from the first salesperson you talk to. Talk to the manager. If that does not help, call the manufacturer's 800 number for customer service. If you have to negotiate to get a store to accept returns, know that they do not have to accept returns at all. Have your receipt and your tags still attached. You may have to settle for store credit or an exchange instead of cash.

Know how to barter goods and services

Bartering, sometimes known as swapping, is trading goods and services without cash. You can trade clothes, shoes, and accessories online at www.RehashClothes.com. They ship their stuff to you and you ship your stuff to them. We have a section in our first book about bartering.

Online, you can swap your used stuff in every category at www.craigslist.com and www.SwapTree.com. To swap your video games, check out www.Gametz.com. To swap your books, use www.PaperBackSwap.com, www.TitleTrader.com, and www.BookMooch.com. For used textbooks, there are also many dedicated websites such as www.TextSwap.com. For CDs, use www.SwapaCD.com. For DVDs there is www.SwapaDVD.com, www.PeerFlix.com, and www.half.ebay.com, which is eBay's non-auction sister site. Everything from appliances to industrial equipment, go to www.toolzdo.com.

Here are some websites for swapping used clothes: Used clothes and fashion accessories can be swapped at www. SwapStyle.com. If you want to borrow or lend stuff, click on www.SnapGoods.com. Use caution when buying or selling used products for children. Avoid used products that have to do with safety, such as car seats, strollers, cribs, crib mattresses, and toys. These should be purchased new so that they meet current safety standards and age appropriateness. Used products that are safe for children are books and clothing. To join the reusing and recycling "freeconomics" community, check out www.freecycle.com.

Note that, on all these sites, you can list the items you're willing to swap or negotiate with the lister of an item that you want. Some of the sites work on a credit system or require membership or a minimal monthly membership fee. Buyers, sellers, and traders are rated online and the community polices itself. If you want someone to do it for you, check out www.I-SoldIt.com.

Know how to barter your services

If someone you meet is skilled in a service that you would like to have, ask that person if he or she would be interested in a "trade" of services. You can swap your services for someone else's services that you want or need. Check out service swapping websites: www.u-exchange.com, www. TradeaFavor.com, www.JoeBarter.com for ideas.

Services can be professional such as legal, medical, dental, or accounting. They can be hobbies such as photography, painting, knitting, crochet, carpentry, refinishing furniture, reupholstery, music lessons, or golf lessons. They can be skills such as editing, calligraphy, or dog training. They can be assistance such as facials, hair cutting, massage, dog walking, house sitting, plant sitting, elder care, or child care. Just decide what skills and talents you have to offer and what skills and talents you are looking for!

Set up your trade properly. Keep track of hours in a way that is fair for both sides. Consider swapping hour for hour to keep track of the traded services. Some practitioners such as personal trainers, Pilates and yoga instructors, and massage therapists have closed their shops to provide their services at their home studios or on-site at their clients' homes or offices. Check with your accountant about possible income tax issues. Initially meet with your swapping colleague in a safe, public location.

If you have a skill that you can charge an hourly rate for and provide it via the Internet, look at outsource sites. You can outsource your talents by signing up to receive referrals to client prospects who are looking for your services. Check out sites such as www.upwork.com, www.fiverr.com, www. elance.com, www.guru.com, and www.peopleperhour.com.

Try competitive bidding

An effective way to save money on major items such as household repairs, car repairs, household remodeling, and other major projects is to use competitive bidding. Competitive bidding is taking a project or a need and asking various suppliers and vendors to bid for the job. Once, Sam and his wife needed carpeting on a stairway and the bids range from $4,000 down to $1,000. They accepted the $1,000 bid and received excellent service. In remodeling his house in Malibu, he saved thousands of dollars by using competitive bidding.

But before you bid, check out your contractor completely. This effort will save time, money, and delays, plus potential legal expenses later. It isn't enough to make sure your contractor is licensed with the state and that no complaints are filed against him. You must also check three or four references and go to his job sites. Your investigation should go even further. Visit him in his office. Check court records for any litigation. Obtain written documentation of his liability and workers compensation policies. Then check out your state's Contractors License Board, the National Association of Remodeling Industry www.nari.org, the Better Business Bureau www.welcome.bbb.org, and Contractors from Hell at www.ContractorsFromHell.com. Read reviews of his workmanship on consumer feedback websites such as www.angieslist.com.

Here is how to conduct competitive bidding:

1. Get bids ONLY from qualified bidders. To be qualified, the bidder must have a good reputation, be financially sound, properly licensed, and supply recommendations that can be cross-verified.
2. Use accurate, detailed specifications. Specifications should be accurate and thorough, so that there is no opportunity for error or misunderstanding. Be specific about materials to be used, so there is no chance of inferior materials. If bidders use substitutions, they must state this in their bid with an explanation.
3. Specify the time for performance.
4. Make sure the bid includes delivery, taxes, license fees, installation, removal, and disposal of items being replaced. The bid must indicate how long it is good for.
5. Treat competitive bidding like shopping. Think of it like comparing vendors and prices before making a final decision. Always get a bid for the entire job rather than simply by the hour or by quantity unless you are specifying a particular quantity.

Try layaway buying

Often you can wait for the clothes but you want to "claim" them now. Ask if the store has a layaway plan. These plans are becoming popular again. You give the store a small down payment to keep the item for you. Then you pay a small amount each week until the item is paid for. This is a good incentive to keep saving and paying until the item is yours. The added beauty is no interest charges.

When Heidi was young, her mother purchased expensive items with a layaway plan. It seemed perfectly normal, while frequent credit card use was not. Weekly payment plans are about delaying ownership, while credit cards are about instant gratification. Recently, stores such as Kmart, Burlington Coat Factory Warehouse, Marshalls, T.J. Maxx and other stores now allow customers to pay over time. To learn more about this new shopping trend and stay in your budget, check out www.elayaway.com.

GARAGE SALE

Illustration by Ros Webb

Illustration by Ros Webb

"You can't afford to feed it, you have no place to keep it, and what will you do with the poop?"

"I couldn't resist! It was such a bargain!!"

Chapter 9

MONEY MIND SET
AND SPENDING ADDICTION

*"Money never makes a man happy yet, nor will it.
The more man has, the more he wants.
Instead of filling a vacuum, it makes one."*

—Benjamin Franklin

ARE YOU ADDICTED TO DEBT? What is it that drives you away from reaching your financial goals and forces you to be a slave to debt? The easiest way to determine whether or not you're addicted to debt is if you find yourself thinking about borrowing for something you do not need. If you have a good job or a steady source of income there is (absent personal catastrophes) no need to be in debt, but many tell themselves that they "need" something that requires them to go into debt, increase their debt, or leads them to take money that had been earmarked to pay down debt, and use it for another purchase.

The most irrational situation is when someone wants to escape from debt takes on more debt to "help him" cope with debt. Among the examples are: Don't purchase a new car when you have a good-running car that is both free and clear or will soon be paid off.

Sam knows people who make good salaries well within a range to keep them comfortable. But they take expensive vacations on borrowed money and return from the trip stressed by the debt they have incurred. Post-vacation stress can cause negative behaviors such as overeating, which undoes the supposed benefit gained from a vacation.

Watch out for an addiction to instant gratification

Credit cards taught us this one: You want it? You have plastic money you can use anytime! The will to resist such temptation has to be learned and taught. It is not part of our original personality.

Parents have an additional responsibility. Not only do they have to learn to control their own "I want it now" tendencies, they owe it to their children to teach them to delay gratification. Stanford University, Sam's alma mater, conducted the famous "marshmallow experiment" in the 1960s. People haven't changed much since. A group of four-year-olds were given one marshmallow and promised a second one on the condition they wait twenty minutes before eating the first one. Some children were able to wait and others could not. The researchers then followed the progress of each child into adolescence and demonstrated that those with the ability to wait were better adjusted and more dependable and scored significantly higher on their college entrance tests years later.

The point is that learning to wait is not something that comes easily, but it's worth it. Things worth having are worth waiting for. "If [children] have everything their heart desires by the time they are 14… what reason do they have to want to grow up?" asks child psychologist Wendy Mogel, author of "The Blessing of a Skinned Knee."

One blogger put it this way: "The relentless focus on having and buying and wanting and owning—and using your credit card or your home equity to cover it—has landed us with crates of things we don't need, stuffed into compartments were we never see it, throwing more money down the drain for the meaningless thrill of knowing we have it." Even if you think you will always have enough money to throw down the drain, now is the time to plug the drain, and unhook from the addiction to instant gratification.

Understand that money is a magnifier

Money is a magnifier. If good things are going on in your life, more money will magnify that good. If there are bad things going on in your life, more money will magnify it. As Dan Millman said,

"Money is neither my god nor my devil. It is a form of energy that tends to make us more of who we already are, whether it's greedy, or loving. If money becomes your god, you can become addicted to it. Or if the things that money can buy become your god, you can become addicted to spending money to get those things. Desire is hardwired. We desire things beyond those necessary to live. But if you constantly crave too much, you will be perpetually disappointed with your life. A survival instinct on overdrive can turn into meaningless excess.

If you are experiencing a spending problem, the single most important words that you must be able to admit freely, openly, and often are "This may be something that I'd love to have, but I can't afford it." If you can afford it, have the confidence to say that you don't need it. You will have to learn to ignore your friends and your own mental urgings when you're tempted to buy something that will move you into debt or move you away from paying down debt. Instead, focus on valuing relationships and financial independence over material things. This is the only way to obtain the things in your life that have positive value. It is the way to a stress-free, happy and contented life.

Take the first steps

The first step in overcoming debt addiction is the same as in any other addiction. You must admit both to yourself and a few special others that you have a problem. Without this admission you are limited in your ability to make sound, unemotional financial decisions.

The second step is to write down a practical plan on how you are going to escape the addiction. Escaping addiction is not easy. A complete change in personal attitudes and values is necessary. Ability to clearly think through wants versus needs, (discussed in our first book), is essential.

Third, realize there is no quick fix that will cure an addiction. Fixes are only temporary and will end up making the problem worse. With addiction there's a cycle of feelings. The euphoria of acquiring new things leads to a sense of dismay as it wears off. This drives you to the next fix of the next acquisition.

Fourth, realize that you can't blame others for your situation. You must accept that the choices are yours, and that if you have a debt financed lifestyle you've made a bad choice.

Fifth, overcome your own deceptions and face up to what you have been doing. Lay out in detail a plan for your life for both the short term and the long term. Recognize value and distinguish what is a desire for something that will provide immediate pleasure but no long term benefit and something that will bring you closer to your goal of financial independence. Know what that goal is and revisit at least once a year.

Eliminate debt

Saving is important and the first step is eliminating debt. As with any goal develop a timeline and objective way of accomplishing it. As seen in all of the literature on attaining financial freedom both small and large steps are necessary. Do not fall into the trap of ignoring the small steps because they build proper habit patterns and financial muscle. Large steps are important as well because they take you forward to your financial independence.

Drinking free coffee at the office and bringing your lunch to the office rather than buying it seems like a small step but it can save thousands of dollars per year. Make a plan to do a dozen or more things each month that don't cost any money such as exercise breaks, museum visits, and volunteer work.

We talk about hundreds of steps in our first book and second book, as well as this book.

After you take on the small things, take on the big things. Keep in mind that big things have hidden costs. For example, a forty thousand dollar car will have much higher insurance costs, license fees, and use more gasoline than the typical twenty thousand dollar car. We all know that the day you drive your new car off the lot, there's a substantial drop in value. Unless the car is a business expense, it's going to cost you sixty more percent in earnings than the sticker price. That sixty percent applies to all the extra cost we've just discussed as well as the purchase itself. Eliminate debt by not going into debt with big things in the first place. See the chapter on taxes in our first book.

Know how much is enough

How much is enough? The answer is different for everyone. The amount of "enough" for you may be less than you think. If you do not feel that you have "enough" you can still think and act with abundance. Give smiles and compliments generously. Counter thoughts of scarcity. Tell yourself, "I have all I need and I have enough to share." Be generous to yourself with things that don't cost money. For example, are you giving yourself enough healthy food, rest, exercise? What about giving yourself encouraging thoughts? A sense of abundance can come from a sense of fulfillment. Fulfillment can come from work you are passionate about. It can come from a simplified way of life. Fulfillment rarely comes from getting material things you already have or don't need.

Illustration by Ros Webb

*"Let's join a cult that has a large group wedding,
to save money."*

Chapter 10

MONEY MIND SET AND BEHAVIOR

"He who has enough and doesn't know it is poor."
—April Benson, Ph.D.

BEHAVIORAL FINANCE is the study of the way you handle money. In other words, what makes you spend or not spend? Behavior finance experts watch consumer spending habits during good times and hard times. They point to an innate "optimism bias" most people have that makes them overly optimistic. We recommend that if your financial situation starts to improve, restrain your optimism bias. Continue to save for that rainy day, even if the storm clouds are only remotely on the horizon. We believe in planning for Murphy's Law, "Whatever can go wrong will." As Sam joked in our first book, "And Murphy was an optimist!"

A *New York Times* article observed, "It takes both a long time and a complex combination of factors—often including some personal trauma, social stigma, and government policy—to promote any real [behavior finance] transformation."

People are good at justifying behavior

Advertisers, financial manipulators, and scammers work overtime devising strategies and techniques to convince us money can buy anything. We let them do it and we do it to ourselves. See if any of these justifications sound familiar:

"This is worth the price." When Sam was representing a developer who was selling membership in a campground, the developer found that membership sales were slow, so he hired a pricing consultant. The consultant suggested only one change: triple the price of the memberships. He explained that the target customers had an imbedded belief that more expensive things were more valuable. To the developer's surprise, the memberships quickly sold out! Confusing price with quality is a characteristic of "behavior finance." In other words, people just naturally do it. Remember this story and know that you don't have to be one of those people.

"This is a great savings." In department stores, items marked down 70% seem like a good deal, whether the product was worth the original price or not. Ask yourself, would you have purchased the item at the original price?

"It's all relative." Sales associates often show customers a house or car above their stated price range before they show them one in their stated price range. Sometimes they start yearning for what they can't afford, now that they've seen it. If they "settle" for something within their price range, they tend to do so with less haggling. This technique also is applied when soliciting donations. You may receive a donation request to donate $1000, $500, $250, $50 or $10. Suddenly, the $10 donation looks small by comparison. Some people feel inclined to donate at least $10, because "After all, it's only $10."

"I felt obligated…" Have you ever been approached by a stranger who offered you a flower or a card and asked you for a donation? Do you feel obligated to make a donation? If a service company offers a free inspection, do you feel obligated to have repairs done with that company, even though if it is more expensive than other companies? Be careful to separate your spending decisions from the fact that you received something free. Evaluate your natural tendency to reciprocate.

"But I said I would…" Sometimes an item is unavailable and a shopper is offered the opportunity to sign a commitment

to purchase it when it becomes available. Be cautious about signing a commitment to buy an item, even if you can return the item or rescind your purchase. You feel compelled psychologically try to follow through with your commitments, even if you change your mind about wanting to buy the item.

People are gullible

We get into trouble because we are susceptible to advertising ploys. Advertisers work overtime to figure out how to get money out of our pockets and into theirs. Here are a few "lines of reasoning" that you may find yourself thinking before you make a purchase. Stop and ask where that thought came from.

"It wasn't the price I first agreed to, but..." Beware of "low-balling" ploys, especially when buying a car. The sales associate may offer a low price first, then discuss it with his or her manager and return with excuses about why the price must be raised. Once you've agreed on a price, stick with it.

"The endorsements really impressed me." They tell you that more people buy this brand than any other... More doctors approve this brand than any other... Most purchasers of this product buy the service contract... My favorite celebrity loves this product... Studies show that half the world population love this product... All my friends are buying this product. Don't be afraid to ask questions and think for yourself before you buy. This trick is called "advertising transference." You transfer your respect for doctors or celebrities to respect for the product.

"It looked great on the mannequin/on the model in the catalog." Clothes always look great on models and mannequins. That's because they are size zero. If the clothes don't look good on them, watch out. They probably won't look better on you! Also watch out for the "transference" technique. Advertisers know that positive feelings about the person in the advertisement are "mentally transferred" to the items being promoted in the advertisement. If the person in the ad is handsome or beautiful,

the clothes they are wearing or the car they are driving looks attractive. To avoid this human tendency to transfer positive feelings from one thing to another, look at the car or the clothes free of the model. Imagine the clothes or car with an unattractive person. Still like it?

"This deal is available today only." Sam automatically says "no" when pressured for an immediate response. He finds expensive items on sale for less later. For example, he buys his suits at the men's section of department stores only during sales.

We've all been victims of these kinds of thoughts. Advertising is very, very effective. Just teach yourself to listen closely to the thoughts that motivate your buying decisions. Remember when your mother taught you to cross the street carefully. She probably taught you the time-honored phrase, "Before you cross the street, Stop, Look, and Listen." We recommend that before you buy, stop and look at your motivations, justifications, and rationalizations for your buying decisions.

People have a "herd" mentality

Retailers know that we lose our judgment when we are in group situations. Know if you have a weakness for being one of the herd. If so, be careful for these danger zones:

"Everyone was at the store, so I found lots of things I wanted to buy there, too." Here is behavior finance at work right before your very eyes: If a store is busy, the merchandise is more likely to sell more quickly and at higher prices. Restaurants have dark lighting to make it look more crowded. Auction houses hire fake shoppers called shills to get the bidding going.

"It was the last one left, so I had to get it." Probably one of the most effective techniques for getting us to purchase something we don't need is to create the perception of scarcity. Think of the news stories of a store announcing it will receive a limited shipment of a new gadget—and devoted shoppers sleep in the store parking lot to be first in line the moment the store opens. "Limited quantities," "only one per customer," and "this

store only," "only for the first ten customers" are phrases that encourage us to buy when we wouldn't usually do so.

"The store was jammed, so I just bought whatever I could find, and got out of there." When a store is crowded, and customers are jostling each other, fingering all the merchandise, and waiting in long lines, it is easy to say to yourself, "I feel distracted and pressured, so I need to make some quick decision without worrying too much about what I'm really buying or really paying."

People can use the "herd mentality" to their advantage

Now that you know about the herd mentality, Sam suggests that you use it to your advantage. For example, if you are trying to sell something, try to gather as many potential buyers as possible. Have them together in the same room. Think "live auction." The synergy in the room increases purchasing motivation and peer pressure. Suddenly, the item starts to seem more desirable. Have you ever participated in a live auction in which you paid much more than you wanted to— for something you didn't even really want?

"Everyone else wanted it too, and I just got caught up in the bidding." The auction version of "The store was jammed" technique is the "everyone else wanted it, too." If an auction is well attended, you are more likely to bid. If others are actively bidding on an item, you may find yourself looking at it with renewed interest.

Aren't you more inclined to patronize a store or restaurant with lots of people in it rather than an empty one? If it is nearly empty, you find yourself wondering what is wrong with the merchandise. If it's crowded, you have the silent vote of many that "this is the place to be." If you are considering buying a house and you know that only one other person has put in a bid in the last two months, you start to wonder if the house is over-priced.

Use this to your advantage. When buying something, find out who your "competition" is. Avoid outside interference, and ask to negotiate in a private environment. Shop on slow, non-weekend days, and at the end of the day when the store doesn't have too many customers. The sales staff will be more attentive, and you will have better results with your haggling, because the store will be trying to reach its daily sales goal.

People invest emotionally, not logically

Another aspect of behavior finance is how we invest. While we don't offer specific investment advice in this book, here are some observations on the market that hold true throughout time about human nature and money:

1. You see the future from your own perspective. If things have always been good for you, you assume that they always will be good. If things have always been bad for you, you assume that they will always be bad.
2. A corollary to number one: Past performance is no indication of future performance. Because something has always been good or bad does not mean that it will continue to be.
3. Professional advisers such as brokers and financial consultants are often wrong. No one likes to admit they're wrong, especially a professional consultant. You can't blame others. The final decision on what happens to your money is yours and yours alone.
4. A corollary to number three: Everyone dislikes admitting mistakes. To correct a mistake is to admit a mistake. Sometimes pride motivates people to choose living with a mistake rather than correcting it. Unfortunately, pride can be a very costly indulgence. If you made a mistake, don't deny it. Admit it, correct it, and get on with your life.
5. People would rather lose with their friends than win

without them. People tend to complain about a particular problem freely—such as falling home and stock values—as long as others are complaining with them. Watch what happens when someone says they have overcome that problem. Rather than receive congratulations, they may get a cool response. If you plan on being successful, be prepared for this flaw in human nature. You can either enjoy your misery with others, or enjoy your success alone. Your choice.

6. The reason we have two ears and one mouth is that we should listen twice as much as we speak. Don't claim to know it all already. Collect as much information as possible from as many sources as possible. Investments should be based on logic, not emotion. Knowledge is the best way to overcome emotion.

People get sluggish brains in an emergency

The book *Unthinkable: Who Survives When Disaster Strikes,* by Amanda Ripley claims that it's better to think about the unthinkable disaster scenarios before they happen rather than after they happen. People's brains tend to move in slow motion in crisis because they are over-stressed. Oxygen and blood rushes to the heart, which is pumped up with adrenaline, leaving the poor brain to muddle along as best it can with limited resources. We think slower and move slower in crisis. This is why poor decisions, sometimes foolishly laughable decisions are made under panic situations.

In a panic situation, get to the "acceptance" stage as quickly as you can. Get beyond rejection, resistance, and denial. Accept the challenge as reality. This will help get your mind calm and working more effectively. If you are working yourself into panic mode through constant worry about a situation, ask yourself the question one of Heidi's attorney friends always asks his new clients: What are you most afraid of in this situation? Your answer may surprise you.

The corollary to the sluggish brain syndrome is human resistance to planning ahead. We are naturally fearful creatures. Fear is survival instinct that can actually threaten our survival. We have to let the analytical part of our brain have the reigns over the emotional side of our brain. Behavior economist George Loewenstein coined the term "the ostrich effect." The ostrich effect is your desire to "stick your head in the sand" when things aren't going well. We recommend that you keep the sand out of your brain and let it do its best work in a positive environment. Face reality and possible "worst case scenarios."

Kent Moyer, president of The World Protection Group, says small changes in attitude and behavior can make a big difference in an emergency. When you sit on the tarmac, look at the evacuation plan brochure. When you enter a building, notice where the exits, stairwells, and fire alarms are. When you enter a room, notice what could fall on you in an earthquake, what you could duck under if you needed to protect yourself, and where you could exit, if you needed to.

Disaster scenarios might be your investments fell in value, your home was threatened with foreclosure, and you lost your job, lost your health, or lost your spouse or significant other. Instead of waiting, think now while things are stable. Ask yourself in a calm moment some "what if" questions. What if the worst were to happen? What options would I have? What could I do now that would provide a buffer? What could I do now that would ensure the worst won't happen? These questions and their answers could make the difference between a crisis becoming an opportunity or a disaster.

People have money scripts

Money scripts are concepts about money that were during childhood from parents and personal experiences. Examine why you do what you do with your money, what are your inner motivations. What do you tell yourself about money?

Some people imitate their parents' money script, such as, "My parents always spent lavishly whether they had money or not. I was raised that way, so that's just the way I am." Another script might read like this: "I never had enough as a child, so I am going to make sure I have everything my heart desires now." Or "I don't pay attention to where my money goes, but somehow, I always manage to get by." Your money script may be unconscious, so don't let it dictate your behavior without your permission. Face up to it and call it out.

Affirming negative things over and over, such as "I am never going to get ahead with my savings; I will never have enough," also can cause problems. We start to see the world from our own perspective and try to make it reality. This can either work against you if what you are claiming is not toward your highest good. Analyze whether your inner money scripts are reasonable, realistic, and heading you in the right direction.

People have money motivations

There are common traits among humans in their behavior about finances. Some negative behaviors interfere with willingness, and therefore ability, to save money. These behaviors are sometimes caused by internal motivations. See if you recognize any of these "money motivations" that prevent you from saving money:

- feeling inadequate
- needing to buy expensive gifts to earn another's love or gratitude
- rewarding yourself for hard work by buying something you don't need
- compensating yourself for a feeling of unworthiness
- filling a sense of loneliness
- looking for a sense of fulfillment in your life
- despairing that your life will ever get better
- rushing to enjoy your life while you can
- following lessons you learned as a child

- repeating your family's tradition of spending
- falling into your old spending habits
- believing that debt is inevitable
- worrying that you're never going to get ahead
- rebelling against authority figures
- compensating for deprivation you endured in your past
- competing with your neighbors, friends, and family
- maintaining a standard of living others expect you to have
- affirming that you deserve "only the very best"
- procrastinating on starting your savings plan
- fearing that you'll fail on your savings plan
- denying that you have a spending problem
- berating yourself that you don't have control
- avoiding the concept of a "budget"
- resisting any limitations on your life
- refusing to admit that the economy is making your life tougher
- creating a reputation of being very generous to others
- fearing that you could be considered poor or cheap
- putting off making difficult choices
- hating to say "no" to those you love or respect

People, just like governments, have difficulty making decisions. Unfortunately, avoidance relinquishes control. Who knows when someone will switch on the lights and announce that the "party" is over? We suggest that you turn on the lights in your own life now and see what there is to see.

Illustration by Ros Webb

"Sorry, sir. I invested it all in apartment buildings."

Chapter 11

MONEY MIND SET: THE SAVER'S BRAIN

*"If a person gets his attitude toward money straight,
It will help straighten out almost every other area of his life."*

—Billy Graham

THERE IS OFTEN a difference between those who appear rich and those who actually have money. Appearances can be deceiving. People who actually have wealth, and not just the appearance of affluence, have learned to handle their money. They know how to save.

Savers aren't smarter, saner, or more energetic than everyone else. They have, however, overcome some of the deep-seated, complicated obstacles to modifying their behavior. Behavior modification, the science of getting yourself to do the things you know you should do, is an art, not a science. You know yourself better than anyone. You know what you need to do to have more success with saving money or any other goal you set for yourself. You know what you need to do; you just have trouble making yourself do it. Our rational mind has to have a discussion with our irrational mind. The self that wants a strong savings account has to reject the self that wants to blow it on a cruise.

We put together our own list of some of the thought-processes that go on behind the brain and pull out aspects of what we call "the saver's brain."

Savers know themselves

Take a sincere look at your spending habits and what motivates you and your finances. Are you ready to stop prolonging higher debt? Are you ready to lay down your credit cards and say "I quit" playing around with the credit-card-shuffle game? Only you know when you are ready.

You may know a few others who are ready to quit, too. One of the ways to help yourself and your friends develop good spending habits is to have "bragging" sessions which emphasize not how much you spent, but how well you've spent and how much you've saved. Develop a saving specialty in a certain area. Know who has expertise in other areas. For example, one of Heidi's areas of expertise is fashion. It is part of "who she is" to dress in style (at reasonable cost). On the other hand, she depends on the advice of people who know cars, when it is time for her to shop for a car. Sam is the go-to-guy for anyone who wants to save money in acquisition and management of real estate. He first learned that he liked to be frugal in his days at Stanford University, where he ran a boarding house and had to plan large dinners and social events at low cost.

Know yourself. If you are naturally frugal, be proud of it!

Savers know which techniques will motivate them

What works for one won't work for everyone. Find a technique for budgeting that works for you. Take a tip from financial planners. These days, financial planners are under increasing pressure to help their clients "get their arms around" their spending. They have to do this in a tactful, but effective way. They turn into part money manager and part family therapist. They have to know their client and what motivates them, and how their incentive centers tick. Easier said than done.

Here are two tactics: The first is short term and intense, the other is long-term and more mild. In the first tactic, you tell yourself that you are going to go on a short, focused program.

Start by recording every expenditure. This makes you more

aware, helps with long-term planning, until budgeting becomes second nature. You can use an old-fashioned notepad, or use expense-tracking applications, such as www.Mint.com and www.QuickenOnline.com. They are free and allow you to keep track of your credit cards, debit cards, and bank accounts so that your spending is automatically documented for you. You can manually add cash spending. This creates a record-keeping system of your expenses so you can analyze your spending. Nevertheless, be cautious about the security issues of sharing your financial information online. Cellphones have less security than personal computers. There is always a price to pay for convenience, and often is the loss of privacy.

If tracking spending long-term creates "budget burnout," you could set a goal of tracking for just a few months. If you stop tracking, remember that you need an update every few months to make sure that expenses haven't swung out of hand again. If you make yourself pay in cash, you have to plan ahead. There is pain in payment with cash. Plastic is painless—until the bill arrives in the mail. The same is true for making yourself write down every expenditure. The annoyance of notating is sometimes enough to make you think twice about spending in the first place.

Savers understand
how retailers manipulate shoppers

Retailers are experts at separating you from your money. You can turn the tables on them! You can build positive reinforcement around the fun of saving, negotiating purchases, and living economically. B.F. Skinner, the eminent psychologist and father of behavior modification would tell you this: whatever you want to become addicted to—make it fun and your job is half done. He documented that positive reinforcement can lead to behavior change. If living **TheSmartestWay** is something that you enjoy, you will seek to do it again and again. Focus on the personal pride you feel as you save money, each day. We push pain away from us and pull pleasure close to us. Make saving pleasurable and you use behavior modification to your advantage.

It's no secret that some people go shopping when they are bored, lonely, or depressed. Shopping can be a diversion from negative feelings. A study by the Carnegie Mellon University found that people tend to spend more money if they are sad. A study at Cornell University found that people in a positive mood did a better job at money problem-solving. Apparently, you need to watch your green when you're blue! The explanation was that sadness increases self-focus, which impaired spending judgment. Boredom and feelings of deprivation are triggers for over-spending, too. In short, work through whatever is preventing you from feeling optimistic, and you'll be a happier person and a better saver.

Retailers know that when we shop tired, confused, rushed, or distracted, we don't analyze our purchases objectively. Don't automatically say "yes." Learn how to say "no" first and "maybe" later. Tell the sales associate politely but firmly that you are going to make a careful decision. Sometimes purchases seems so complex, you may be tempted to be make a decision in a hurry. The more expensive the transaction, the more time you need to make the right decision. Successful sales associates are trained to sell by their warmth, personalization, and their "special" offers.

Retailers email you reminders, showing you ticking time clocks on limited merchandise so you do not miss that can't-live-without item, and offer additional incentives like free shipping if you make just one more purchase. (They already know what you like, because they have been carefully electronically documenting your buying habits.) The websites make payment a breeze by inserting your credit card information for you, and for your convenience, setting you up with their "Bill Me Later" feature. What could be easier than clicking the "yes" button? For those of us who like to shop carefully, they offer generous guarantees and free return shipping. They know that after you receive the merchandise, you will not be motivated to return it. If you just window shop and put things in your cart and leave the site, they make sure your cart is still full whenever you return. If you are a loyal customer, you are rewarded with further incentives, mark-downs and upgrades that "regular" shoppers do not receive. They make you feel like you are in an elite group. They make you feel special.

Here are three ways to resist the shopping siren call, both online and in person:

1.   Carry your shopping list and stick with it. Online, do not let coupons and free-shipping minimums peel away your good intentions. In person, skip the shopping cart if possible. Go straight to your designated aisle; do not stop and touch other items. Ignore the impulse items at the checkout stand. When you get to the checkout and realize you are overspending, simply hand the extra items to the cashier and say politely, "I am not buying this today." Heidi does it all the time, and no cashier has ever fainted.

2.   Make payment a hassle. In person, bring cash in an envelope, and do not use a credit card or debit card. Online, do not let retailers store your information. Type it all in every time. Double check the balance. Look for coupon codes to reduce the price. Refuse to be rushed. It took time to earn it; it should take time to spend it.

3.   Make you, your money, and your time inaccessible. Get off catalog mailing lists by writing on the catalog Return to Sender and handing it back to the postal carrier. Remove your name from online retailers' alerts lists and payment plans. Sure, you will be ignorant of some bargains, but your wallet will be unaware blissfully.

Savers have their priorities straight

It has been said that "Money won't buy happiness, but it will pay the salaries of a huge research staff to study the problem," or "Money can't buy friends, but you can get a better class of enemy." It's more difficult to joke about the fact that money doesn't buy happiness at times when money is tight. It does, however, give an opportunity to re-evaluate what is really important in life. Money is less important to one's level of happiness than deep relationships and satisfaction with one's accomplishments.

There is a phrase that a good life is made up of earning, learning, and yearning. All three work together: yearning motivates us to learn and earn and we can't earn without learning. True love, lasting loyalty, deep respect, and genuine friendship can only be earned, not purchased. Good taste, good manners, a good education, and the ability to live life joyfully can only be learned, not purchased.

It takes real skill and concentration to pick things which will provide a sense of satisfaction, accomplishment, fun in life and help you reach your goals. Some activities require effort and concentration which makes is uncomfortable, but the rewards of improving far outweigh the effort.

What are you really yearning for in life? Sam found an article in the Jewish Journal several years ago entitled, "The Answer is Love," It is an excerpt from *More Money Than God: Living a Rich Life Without Losing Your Soul,* by Steven Z. Leder. In it, Leder recounts being called to the bedside of a man he had never met, "an extremely famous and wealthy movie director." The elderly gentleman struggled to lift his oxygen mask and asked in a whisper, "What is it all for?" Searching how to answer the gentleman, he glanced at the very old, small photograph tacked on the hospital wall. It was a picture of a young couple holding hands on a park bench. "It's to love and be loved," he told him. "They understood that," he said pointing to the picture.

With all of his success, the gentleman was dying alone, asking a stranger what life was really about. Leder concluded that he believed, "A life well-lived is filled with love given and received... No matter what our net worth... we can all invest in and achieve the wealth of friendship…We can all lead richer lives, ever more grateful simply to love and be loved."

Savers are optimistic

No one is optimistic non-stop. It's not "all good" all the time. When times are difficult and you have to make hard choices, it's easy to get down-hearted. However, people who lead others, heads of organizations, businesses, or government, present a "can-do" attitude in order to be successful in their endeavors. You could say, "When the going gets tough, the tough get going." When times are down, the upbeat keep moving ahead.

Sam doesn't advocate complaining. He says it is a waste of time and unproductive. Heidi, on the other hand, has found that being in touch with her feelings is healthy. She acknowledges when she's not feeling optimistic and takes a close look. Are feelings of "depression" actually anger, frustration, or disappointment? About what? Find the problems that are the root of the negative feelings. Jot down some action steps to solve them. This little exercise reduces stress remarkably. Less stress is good for your health.

Sometimes, you need to feel sorry for yourself for a few minutes. Heidi knows if it seems like a pity party is brewing, she just gives in to it, rather than spend too much energy fighting it. The key to pity parties, is to keep them short. It's not if you indulge, it's how you indulge. There is an old saying, "Life is too short for long pity parties." After the pity party (which no one wants to attend with you), the reality is that to be successful in life, you have to get up, dress up, and show up. No one can do that for you.

Savers know they must keep telling themselves that their efforts will be worthwhile in the long-term. They stay positive about their future prospects.

Savers aren't perfectionists

This is a hard one for Heidi. Editors have to watch out for "perfectionitis" in their personal goals. Sam constantly warns Heidi about this. Perfectionism may be helpful in our professional lives, but when you are dealing with your own goals and falling short of them frequently, a phrase that works is: "I am not a perfectionist, I am a progressionist." Progress is the goal, not perfection. Perfection is a quickly moving target. Life happens and it always will. What seems like a perfect scenario today may not be tomorrow. Adaptability is not an excuse, it is a survival mechanism. It will help you keep your balance. If you do well on one day toward your savings goals, congratulate yourself. Do not berate yourself if you fall short the next day. That will just make you feel discouraged. Heidi tells herself, "Okay, I fell short, but I have to get back up and start again to where I left off. It was just a temporary delay. The only direction I can go is forward."

Is the cost of perfection worth it? An example of perfectionism is "over-improving" a house beyond what increases the house's value. Over-decorating is an expensive indulgence, in an attempt to reach a "perfect" living environment. Heidi recalls viewing a home for sale that had wallpaper on every wall throughout the house. The wallpaper was expensive, but now outdated. She asked if it had added anything to the value of the house.

Do not let yourself invest in time and money wasters that attempt to achieve "perfection"—a state that doesn't actually exist in the first place. Sam says that perfectionists are often procrastinators who seldom complete major goals. "Do the best you can in the time allotted and move on," is one of his secrets of success.

Savers know their "triggers"

Know what triggers your inclination to spend when you shouldn't. Savers guard against them. Compulsive shoppers have many triggers and often they know they need help.

Are you more inclined to take a stroll around the mall when you are feeling bored? The mall provides plenty of sensory opportunities. It is difficult, however, to just look and not touch. When you touch for too long, it is hard to not take ownership. If you try it on, you are more likely to buy it. There are lots of busy people at the mall, so it might make you feel less lonely. A salesperson will be glad to be friendly and even tell you that that sweater looks great on you. Or is shopping an escape, a chance to buy those amazing pair of shoes that will change the way others look at you? Are you looking for a whole new way of looking, living, acting, being? Advertisements promise to make that a reality. What about the surge of optimism that a fresh paycheck gives you? Does money equal power—spending power? Does that money burning a hole in your pocket make you feel independent? Do you want to prove to everyone that you can spend your money any way you choose? Maybe you wait until the last minute to buy a gift, so you are in a rush, even annoyed, and you just buy whatever grabs your attention at the moment, with little thought about the financial consequences.

When you feel your triggers getting pulled, stop and ask why you feel the way you feel. Shopping and spending more money than you have won't cure whatever is bugging you. Sad but true. There are so many other things to do besides spend money. You can think of a few positive alternatives. Exercise, for example. It makes you feel good. But it is good for you, unlike shopping.

Savers are adaptable

Savers are willing to try new things to achieve desired results, even if they feel uncomfortable. Reason wins the day. Gary Belsky and Thomas Gilovich wrote in their book on behavior economics, *Why Smart People Make Money Mistakes—and How to Correct Them,* "Change is often hard-won. There's a reason, after all, why the majority of Weight Watchers members have been through the program before. Actually, the Weight Watchers analogy is particularly apt for the challenge you face in trying to give order to your financial decision-making processes. One of the difficult challenges in trying to change one's diet is that—unlike, say, smoking—you can't just stop cold turkey. You have to eat something. Similarly, you can't stop spending or investing or saving while you rethink the way you make financial decision. You have to change course while in flight."

Sometimes the mid-flight change in direction feels like a jolt. We all have heard of stories of people selling their car, moving back in with family, or eliminating television, Internet, and cell phone service. These detours do not have to get you off track. They can be "an ends to a means" of getting back on your feet financially, starting over, and doing it better the next time around.

Savers understand the concept
of lost opportunity cost

As we mentioned in the first chapter, there is a lost opportunity cost for money. When you spend money, you are not only swapping that money for something. You also are giving up what that money could do for you in any other scenario, or what it could do for you in a future scenario. When considering any major expenditure or ongoing expenditure, stop and evaluate opportunity cost that is, what the alternative is you can do with that expenditure.

Here is a vivid example: Sam had a client who desperately wanted to own her own home and had set aside savings and was only $30,000 short of the necessary down payment. She could save the $30,000 she needed over the next four years with her income. She owned a car she had bought new and financed over five years. Now it was paid off and she owned it free and clear. The car was an SUV which enabled her to carry her dog around and could be used in her profession and had very low mileage. It was in excellent condition and would have lasted at least another seven years.

Instead of hanging onto her current car, she allowed a sales associate at a car dealership to convince her to trade it in as a down payment on a new car. Even worse, she wouldn't even own the new car—she got a lease. Then she paid $500 a month lease payments, without acquiring any equity in the car. The lease payments and the high insurance cost which she incurred over the next four years added up to more than the down payment on a home.

When Sam explained this to her, she was crushed when she realized that she had thrown away her opportunity both to own her own home... and had to start over on car payments. This mistake may have been made by someone you know, or even yourself. Car sales associates are well trained to convince you that a new, status car will improve your life. They are not trained to help you "do the math" about how much your new car will cost you in lost opportunity to fulfill your long-term dreams.

Another client of Sam's had a well-paying job, but bought a home beyond his means. He choose to go a step up beyond his comfort level, even though he had enough money saved to buy a suitable home with cash. On the other hand, the mortgage on the big home he bought, was dependent on his high income. In the economic downturn, he lost his job, and then he lost his house. In the process, he lost the down payment on the house and all the equity. The opportunity to have something he could afford and own forever was blown and it will take him a number of years to recover that opportunity again, assuming that he can find another high-paying job. If he had considered opportunity costs and bought a less expensive property which he could carry on a lesser income, he would still have his own home today.

As we have seen in **TheSmartestWay to Save,** one-time expenditures on ego, luxury items, or impulse gratification often mean losing the chance to acquire something of a real long-term value that will provide pleasure or security for the rest of one's life.

Resist the impulse to buy something beyond your means, a new car or larger home, in order to "keep up with the Jones." You may be keeping up with them, but they may be going downhill, and you may not be far behind! You may be sorely tempted to buy a short-term pleasure, an "ego" purchase, or something that others may urge you to buy that you don't need. Compare that item with what your real long-term goals are and see if you are willing to forego buying it.

Savers know they can become millionaires

Sam has observed that many people who started out in life with very little and become wealthy on a relatively modest income did so simply by spending less than what they earn. One of his best investments is a property purchased more than thirty years ago. The property never increased more than 4% or 5% a year, but the magic of compound interest over time raised the annual income produced by the property to more than he originally paid for the property.

You may not find the following practices easy or fun, but apparently, they seem to work. Many millionaires had parents who did not provide economic "outpatient care" or bail them out of financial difficulties. Nevertheless, they became very wealthy. It all starts from mindset: they are willing to forego the display of high social status in exchange for true financial independence. This mindset guides them to live well below their means and allocate their resources (time, energy, and money) efficiently to build wealth. In their personal lives, they train their children to become economically self-sufficient. In their financial dealings, they are proficient in targeting market opportunities. In their careers, they choose occupations that would garner real wealth, not just prestige.

Thomas J. Stanley, in *The Millionaire Next Door,* points out that many millionaires choose to live in a neighborhood and in a home which is below that which they can afford, enabling them to save and invest towards financial independence. Many of them started from little and still live simply. They do not live in wealthy neighborhoods, they live next door. They do not exhibit affluent lifestyles, even thought they could well afford to do so. Hard work, planning, perseverance, and self-discipline are their secrets, he writes. Saving requires those qualities: working hard to make extra money, planning to put money away, perseverance to stay on track, and self-discipline to avoid the temptation to overspend.

Sounds simple. As everyone knows all too well, simple is not easy. They live with simple, directed focus and a larger purpose. By saving carefully, they gained control of their money and lives.

Savers conquer the goal-setting demon

Everyone knows that goal setters are more likely to succeed than those who do not set goals. If your goal is to save money, you must have a plan it to make it happen. Take positive steps to implement the techniques in our series—this book, **TheSmartestWay™ to Save—Why You Can't Save Money and What To Do About It** and **TheSmartestWay™ to Save More, Making the Most of Your Money.**

It comes down to making different decisions every day. When you find you're procrastinating and making excuses, take some small action toward your goal. Break your action plan down into smaller steps so that it seems easy.

Goal reaching is tougher than goal setting. Be careful to not sabotage your goals. Be patient with yourself. A slow down or slip up is not a reason to quit. We all have negatives that we need to minimize, so focus on maximizing your positives. This is a marathon, not a sprint. But it will never happen if you don't start with the first small step.

Every goal amounts to a bunch of smaller goals. For example, we write our books one chapter at a time. We then broke that down to what we want to cover in a chapter, and then we focus on that list, one item at a time. There are always more things we want to do—workshops, media promotion, research for other books—but none of these will get the book finished. We need focused action—on writing those chapters—if we want to produce a book.

Savers understand inertia

Inertia is the principle in physics that a body at rest stays at rest; a body in motion stays in motion. If you don't start saving, you won't start. Once you start, it is easier to keep going. Simple concept, but how to get started? Don't start with too big a goal and get discouraged. If you start with a small, simple, no-brainer goal, at least you will get started—and inertia will start working for you instead of against you. If you don't know where to start, start at the easiest, most convenient place. If fear of numbers is your problem, keep it simple. Start saving 3 percent of every paycheck. When that gets easy, start saving 5 percent. And keep increasing as often as possible.

Just as life is a journey, accomplishing goals is a journey. You must view the process that way, and learn to recognize the small successes and results that you are making.

Cutting out minor expenditures results, over time, in substantial savings. We mentioned in our first book the Debtors Anonymous "12-Step Program" used to fight many addictions. You must live "one day at a time" and set some small action every day towards your goal. Be sure that it is a simple enough action that can be accomplished within the time you have for it, and don't worry when you miss it. Don't look backwards; simply continue to look towards your goal. Don't stop and let inertia work against you. Keep going and let your momentum work for you.

Savers have inner confidence

Throughout our books we discuss the concept of keeping up with the Joneses. The Joneses represents the people—the neighbors, co-workers, family, and friends—that you think of when you ask yourself, "But what will 'people' think??" What will they think when you refuse to buy things you cannot afford or don't need—just to look like you have the same standard of living that they do?

Not needing to keep up with other people's lifestyle and expenditures is maturity. Younger people are especially vulnerable to peer pressure, societal influence to do the things that they normally wouldn't do. When we grow up, we are supposed to learn to stand on our own two feet, think for ourselves, and not be swayed by the opinions of others. We do what we think is right, even when we expect "push back." This is part of being an adult, learning to withstand the emotional pressure, the embarrassment, or fear of disapproval from others. People don't respect those who waste their resources and overspend.

Do you have a reputation for buying the most expensive gifts or paying for dinner whenever you go out with friends? Earn a reputation for looking good without spending top prices, finding great deals on cars, housing, and other major expenses that won't bust your budget.

You want to earn respect, not envy, right? On the other hand, if you want people to envy you, not respect you, what is behind that desire? If you feel envious of someone who has more than you do, remember W.C. Field's remark, "A rich man is nothing but a poor man with money."

Envy is an indication of low self esteem. Inner confidence means high self esteem. Everyone has self-esteem "issues" from time to time. That is self-damage you don't need. Studies show that people with low self-esteem have trouble saying "no" to temptations to buy. Therefore, there is a double benefit because to boost your self-image is to also boost your savings!

Savers honor their resources

Humans have five sources of power: their time, energy, talent, money, and relationships. All sources of our power are to be cherished. They are not unlimited. All have value, each in their own way. Each can be translated into money, if used appropriately and wisely.

Waste not; want not, was a phrase Heidi grew up with. In any case, wasting is bad. Avoid things, people, and activities that suck power. Like the old refrigerator in the garage holding a six-pack of soda and sucking more than its share of the power supply. Some have a skill for monopolizing our time with needless interruptions. Others can sap our emotions with constant tales of mishaps, poor judgment, and requests for loans.

Be conscious of the importance of valuing your resources, matter how little you have. Be a wise and faithful steward of your time, energy, heart, relationships, and money, to do the most good for yourself, your family, and your community.

CONCLUSION

We hope this book has given you a new perspective and some useful tips on how to manage and enjoy the large things in life for less! Our wish is for you to develop a "saver's brain," save more, spend less and develop your option to achieve financial independence!

We look forward to your comments, suggestions, and feedback!

HEIDI'S PRINCIPLES FOR GAINING CONTROL OF YOUR LIFE —AND YOUR MONEY

"There are three ingredients in the good life:
learning, earning, and yearning."
—Christopher Morley

1. **Say "maybe" before you say "yes."** Don't over-commit; you can always say yes later. Don't be the person everyone expects to come through 100%. This is also true for lending money.

2. **Don't shop until you have a sufficient list.** Keep lists for all of your favorite stores. Build the lists for several months. When there is a sale, or you just can't wait any longer, re-write the list. Then consider where you truly need to shop.

3. **Buy only what you can afford.** When you get to the store, with your list, get your cart and designate two areas: the must-haves and the optional. Put the must-haves on the check-out counter first and keep a running tab until you reach your cash budget.

4. **Use Other People's Energy (OPE).** Put your goals in alignment with others so they will help you reach your goals. Help them coincide with yours so you can reach mutually beneficial goals together and share your motivation and encouragement with each other. This works for setting family budgets, too.

5. **Set limits.** Boundaries are for self-protection, to prevent unnecessary chaos. Have a safe place for your money in your home. Do not allow children to take money from your wallet or handbag.

6. **Honor your time; it has worth.** Delegate tasks to others to give yourself more time to make more money.

7. **Figure out what you really want.** If you don't know what you want, no one can give it to you. You may not truly desire more stuff. Dig deep to find your true heart's desires. Then make a list of the things that don't cost money.

8. **First things first.** Pay yourself first. Do financial must-dos first. Do the harder things in life—like paying the bills—earlier in the day, while you are still fresh and have a good attitude. Added bonus: You will make fewer mistakes.

9. **Keep a calendar.** Do not be late on bills, taxes, important financial duties. Being late costs unnecessary fees and hurts your credit score. Note the important financial dates on your calendar weeks in advance and start preparing early.

10. **Teach your family the concept of balance.** Many families seem entirely focused on the children's schedule and financial desires. Nevertheless, children can be taught to "take turns" in sharing the family's time and money resources with each member of the family. For example, you can say, "Yesterday was your day. Today is Mommy Day." Provide a priceless role model to your children of how to balance everyone's needs while living within your income.

Be sure to review Sam's list of 26 Principles of Financial Independence in our first book and 29 Principles of Financial Independence in our second book.

ABOUT THE AUTHORS

SAM FRESHMAN

Sam Freshman is an attorney, real estate developer, business owner, investor, lecturer, and author. His company, Standard Management Co., manages more than $400 million of real estate assets and business enterprises. His book, **Principles of Real Estate Syndication,** is considered the landmark work on the subject. Clients pay up to $5,000 for his customized workshops and personal coaching on behavioral attitudes that create success. See www.standardmanagement. com and www.syndicationideas.com.

HEIDI CLINGEN

Heidi Clingen has been a journalist, editor, and writer for the past 25 years, including positions at *Apparel News Group* and *The Wall Street Journal,* where she received a Dow Jones Foundation Fellowship. Heidi earned a bachelor's degree in journalism from San Francisco State University, and a screenwriting certificate from UCLA. She devotes her time to researching and speaking on how to live well on a modest income.

WE OFFER COACHING!

We offer workshops, seminars, and training programs for groups of all ages and sizes, as well as one-on-one coaching sessions. Contact us at Heidi@TheSmartestWay.com to tell us how we can help!

ALSO BY SAMUEL K. FRESHMAN
AND HEIDI E. CLINGEN

TheSmartestWay™ to Save
Why You Can't Hang Onto Money
and What To Do About It

TheSmartestWay™ to Save More
—Making the Most of Your Money

ALSO BY SAMUEL K. FRESHMAN
Principles of Real Estate Syndication
with Entertainment and Oil-Gas Syndication
Supplements
3rd Edition

These books are available at
www.Amazon.com,
www.BarnesandNoble.com,
and your local bookstore.

COMING SOON:
Never Be Old Enough To Know Better
—And You Will Be successful in Life and Business

IF WANT TO INVEST YOUR SAVINGS, READ THIS BOOK!

Principles of Real Estate Syndication
(3rd Edition)

By Samuel K. Freshman

Known throughout the real estate industry as the definitive how-to guide, **Principles of Real Estate Syndication** is filled with examples and illustrations of all aspects of buying property with others. This reference guide thoroughly explains the theory and practice of this time-honored way to invest in real estate. Here are some of the many comments posted about this book on Amazon:

"...This book could be titled, how to build a real estate empire. The book provides practical information and advice on avoiding common mistakes..."

"...Comprehensive and authoritative, a must-read for anyone who contemplates investing in a syndication or becoming a syndicator... A treasure trove of information...."

"...A hands-on book, well-written, easy to comprehend, and offers the reader a strategic insight into a complex business form... Should be a permanent fixture in every office..."

Other comments include:

"...This is the instruction manual for this type of venture—a compelling synthesis of practical and technical advice and legal analysis. I recommend the book to anyone involved in real estate or other syndications—attorneys, accountants, bankers, investors, syndicators, students, and more."

"...If you are serious about making money in real estate, read this book. ...This book explains in simple and easy-to understand language the preparation, execution, and practices that must be taken to become successful in the field..."

"...I truly believe this book, if properly followed, can make anybody who reads it substantial amounts of money..."

"...There are dozens of real estate investing books out there, but this is clearly the best I've found..."

Sam has a distinguished career in real estate and law, as an advisor, developer, and investment partner. He is Chairman Emeritus of Stanford Professionals in Real Estate (SPIRE). He is past Chairman of the Legal and Accounting Committee of the California Real Estate Association Syndication Division. He assisted in the preparation of the California Corporation and Real Estate Commissioner's syndicate regulations. In 1961, he formed Standard Management Co., which has sponsored hundreds of millions of dollars of investments in real estate projects throughout the country. You can purchase **Principles of Real Estate Syndication,** 3rd Edition at your local bookstore or Amazon.com.

HOW YOU CAN GET INVOLVED!

HELP US LAUNCH
TheSmartestWay™ Project!

Many worthwhile organizations have asked us for help with financial literacy training. As a result, we are establishing *TheSmartestWay™* **Project** to make our savings books available at cost to qualified organizations that operate homeless shelters, battered women shelters, food pantries, and inner-city schools, as well as financial literacy programs at banks and credit unions. It is our intention that our books, educational programs, and our good will can help adults and teens who are struggling financially. We invite you to contact us at Heidi@TheSmartestWay.com about programs that you would like to receive our books.

TELL US YOUR STORY!

We were proud to share all the stories and essays that the readers of our first book sent in! Now, we would love to hear YOUR story about how you save money! If you email us at Heidi@TheSmartestWay.com a brief, 500 word essay, it may be included in an upcoming book. Please join our expanding community of sensational savers. We look forward to hearing from all of you!

SUGGESTED READING

BUDGETING

1,001 Things They Won't Tell You, An Insider's Guide To Spending, Saving, and Living Wisely,
Jonathan Dahl and the editors of *SmartMoney Magazine*

10,001 Ways To Live Large On A Small Budget,
Writers of Wise Bread

Control Your Cash, Greg McFarlane and Betty Kincaid

Making The Most of Your Money In Tough Times,
Kerby Anderson

Managing My Money, Banking and Budgeting Basics,
Natalie Hales

Money For Life and Money For Life Success Planner,
Steven B. Smith

Pay It Down, From Debt To Wealth On $10 A Day,
Jean Chatzky

Personal Finance For Dummies, Sheryl Garrett

Ten-Day Money Makeover, David R. Hooper

The 1-2-3 Money Plan, Gregory Karp

The Budget Kit: The Common Cents Money Management Workbook, Judy Lawrence

The Money Workbook, Roger Bruce Lane, Ph.D.

Thirty Days To Tame Your Finances,
Deborah Smith Pegues

Your Budget: How To Deal With Money,
Parenting Success Guide

CARS

50 Things To Know Before Buying A Used Car,
Amanda Walton

Buying A Used Car For Dummies, Deanna Sclar

Car Buyer's and Leaser's Negotiating Bible,
W. James Bragg

Car Shopping Made Easy, Jerry Edgerton

Consumer Reports New Car Buying Guide 2014,
  Editors of *Consumer Reports*
Getting The Best Price On A Used Car, Lynette Hartwig
Insider's Guide To Buying A New Or Used Car,
  Burke Leon
Inspect It, Used Car Buying Made Easy, Alan Segel
***Kelley Blue Book* Used Car Consumer Edition,**
  Kelley Blue Book

CHILDREN AND MONEY MINDSET

1,000 Best Baby Bargains, Kimberly Danger
A Smart Girl's Guide To Money, Nancy Holyoke
A Smart Girl's Guide To Money, Nancy Holyoke
  and Bridgett Barrager
Allowance Magic, David McCurragh
Baby Bargains, Denise Fields
Can I Have Some Money!, Candi Sparks
Can I Have Some Money, Please?, Twyla Prindle,
  Dori Miller and Randy Jennings
Debt-Proof Your Kids, Mary Hunt
How To Make Money Sense To Children, Michael Searls
How To Make Your Child Money Savvy, Stuart Fish
How To Teach Your Child About Money, Anza Goodbar
It's A Money Thing, A Girl's Guide To
  Managing Money, Susan Estelle Kwas
Kids & Money: Giving Them The Savvy To
  Succeed Financially, Jayne A Pearl
Kids Clothes For Under $5, Donna Lawson
Little Critter: Just Saving My Money, Mercer Mayer
Making Allowance: A Dollars and Sense Guide
  To Teaching Kids About Money, Paul Lemitte
Making Money, A How-To For A Smart Girl,
  Apryl Lundsten & Brigette Barrager

Money Doesn't Grow On Trees: A Parent's Guide To Raising Financially Responsible Children, Neale S. Godfrey and Carolina Edwards

Money Sense For Kids, Hollis Page Harmon

My Book of Money, Dollars and Cents, Kumon Publishing

My First Book of Money, Kumon Publishing

Neale S. Godfrey's Ultimate Kids Money Book, Neil S. Godfrey

Not Your Parent's Money Book, Jean Chatzky

On My Own Two Feet: A Modern Girl's Guide To Personal Finance, Manisha Thakor and Sharon Kedar

Raising Financial Fit Kids, Joline Godfrey

Raising Money Smart Kids, Ron Blue

Raising Money-Smart Kids: What They Need To Know About Money and How To Tell Them, Janet Bodnar

Silver Spoon Kids, How Successful Parents Raise Responsible Children, Eileen Gallo and Jon Gallo

The Everything Kids Money Book, Brett McNorther

The Complete Book of Baby Bargains, Kimberly Danger

The Financially Intelligent Parent: Eight Steps To Raising Successful, Generous, Responsible Children, Eileen Gallo and Jon Gallo

The Kids Money Book, Jamie Kyle McGillian

The Money Tree Myth, A Parent's Guide, Gail Vaz-Oxlade

The New Totally Awesome Money Book For Kids, Arthur Bochner

Your Kids Can Master Money: Fun Ways To Help Them Learn How, Ron Blue

CLUTTER

1,001 Timely Tips For Clutter Control, The Editors of FC&A Publishing

Enough Already! Clearing Mental Clutter To Become The Best You, Peter Walsh

**From Clutter To Clarity: Simplifying Life From
    Inside Out,** Nancy Twigg
**Give It Up: My Year of Learning To Live Better
    With Less,** Mary Carlmagno
It's All Too Much, Peter Walsh
**Knowing What To Keep, When To Toss, and How To
    Store Your Stuff; Living With Less: The Upside
    of Downsizing,** Mark Tabb
**Shed Your Stuff, Change Your Life: A Four-Step Guide
    To Getting Unstuck,** Julie Morgenstern
**The Boomer Burden: Dealing With Your Parents'
    Lifetime Accumulation of Stuff,** Julie Hall
The One-Minute Organizer: A to Z Storage Solutions,
    Donna Smallin
**Throw Out 50 Things: Clear The Clutter, Find
    Your Life,** Gail Blanke

COLLEGE ON A BUDGET

1,000 Best Smart Money Secrets for Students,
    Debbie Fowles
100 Ways To Cut The High Cost of Attending College,
    Michael Voillt
**Debt-Free U: How I Paid For An Outstanding College
    Education Without Loans, Scholarships or
    Mooching Off My Parents,** Zac Bissonnette
Don't Tell Me What To Do, Just Send Money,
    Helen E. Johnson
**Financial Basics: Money Management Guild
    For Students,** Susan Knox
**Life Happens: Saving On College, Divorce, Hospital
    and Funeral Expenses,** Gregory Karp
Money Management For College Students,
    Larry Burkett
Pay For College Without Sacrificing Your Retirement,
    Tim Higgins

Paying For College Without Going Broke, Kalman Chany
Please Send Money: A Financial Survival Guide
   For Young Adults On Their Own, Dara Duguay
Strapped: Why America's 20- and 30-Somethings
   Can't Get Ahead, Tamara Draut

COUPLES/MARRIAGE PARTNERS
AND MONEY MINDSET

Complete Financial Guide For Young Couples,
   Larry Burkett
Conscious Spending For Couples, Deborah Knuckey
Couples and Money, Marlow Felton
Debt-Proof Your Marriage: How To Achieve
   Financial Harmony, Mary Hunt
Divorce and Money, Violet Woodhouse
Financial Infidelity: Seven Steps To Conquering
   The #1 Relationship Wrecker, Dr. Bonnie Eaker Weil
Financial Intimacy: How To Create A Healthy
   Relationship With Your Money and Your Mate,
   Jacquette M. Timmons
For Love and Money, Debra Kaplan
For Richer Not Poorer, Ruth Hayden
Get Financially Naked: How To Talk Money With
   Your Honey, Tanisha Thakor, Sharon Kedar
Love and Logic Moneyisms, Jim Fay
Love, Marriage and Money, Matt Bell
Money Before Marriage, Larry Burkett
Money Harmony, Olivia Mellan
Money Without Matrimony, Sheryl Garrett
Money, A Love Story: Untangle Your Financial Woes,
   Kate Northrup
Our Money Ourselves For Couples, Diane Ealy, Ph.D.
The Couple's Guide To Love and Money, Jonathan Rich
The Secret Language of Money, David Krueger

The Young Couple's Guide To Growing Rich Together,
Jill Gianola
What To Do Before "I Do," Nihara Choudhri

DECORATING ON A BUDGET

Budget Home Decorating Tips, James Driscoll
Cheap Home Makeover, Caitlin Raur
**City Chic: An Urban Girl's Guide To Decorating
On A Shoestring,** Nina Willdorf
**Country Living: 750 Great Ideas For Decorating
On A Budget,** Nancy Soriano
DIY Home Decorating, Kathy Burns-Millyard
**Easy Does It: Cheap and Simple Ways To Solve
Common Household Problems,**
the editors of FC&A Publishing
**Extraordinary Uses For Ordinary Things
(Vol. I and Vol. II),** editors of *Reader's Digest*
Home Décor On A Budget, Heather Lane
Home Decorating On A Budget, Clara Taylor
How To Decorate On A Budget, Anne Marie Roberts
Interior Design On A Budget, Tommy Ellis
More Splash Than Cash, Donna Babylon
Thrifty Chic: Interior Style On A Shoestring,
Liz Bauwens and Alexandra Campbell

DEBT REDUCTION

**Debt Is Slavery: and Nine Other Things I Wish My Dad
Dad Had Taught Me About Money,** Michael Mihalik
Debt-Free Forever, Gail Vaz-Oxlade
Debt-Proof Living, Mary Hunt
**How To Get Out of Debt, Stay Out of Debt
and Live Prosperously,** Jerrold Mundis
I Haven't Saved a Dime, Now What?!, Barbara Loos
**Life or Debt: A Ten-Week Plan For A Lifetime
of Financial Freedom,** Stacy Johnson

Life Without Debt, Bob Hammond

Master Your Debt: Slash Your Monthly Payments and Become Debt Free, Jordan E. Goodman with Bill Westrom

The Complete Cheapskate: How To Get Out of Debt, Stay Out of Debt and Break Fee From Money Worries Forever, Mary Hunt

The Complete Idiot's Guide To Getting Out of Debt, Ken Clark

The Simple Dollar: How One Man Wiped Out His Deb and Achieved The Life of His Dreams, Trent Hamm

FAMILIES ON A BUDGET

250 Personal Finance Questions For Single Mothers: Make and Keep A Budget, Get Out of Debt, Susan Reynolds

America's Cheapest Family Gets You Right On The Money: Your Guide To Living Better, Spending Less, and Cashing In On Your Dreams, Steve and Annette Conomides

Be Centsable: How To Cut Your Household Budget In Half, Chrissy Pate and Kristin McKee

Bonnie's Household Budget Book, Bonnie Runyan McCullough

Budget On A Shoestring, Nancy Ayres

Family and Friends—From Serial Borrowers To Serious Cheapskates, Jeanne Fleming and Leonard Schwarz

Family Budget Demystified, Bonnie Ruynan McCullough

Going Broke: Why Americans Can't Hold On To Their Money, Stuart Vyse

Half-Price Living: Secrets of Living Well On One Income, Ellie Kay

How To Care For Your Parents' Money While Caring For Your Parents, Sharon Burns

**How To Create and Get Everyone In Your Home
To Stick To A Family Budget,** Brently Clemantin
How To Set Up A Family Budget, Judy Goldberg
I Just Want My Kids To Be Happy, Aaron Cooper
**Isn't It Their Turn To Pick Up The Check?
Dealing With All of The Trickiest Money Problems,**
Jenny Fleming
Miserly Moms, Jonnie McCoy
**Miserly Moms: Living Well On Less In A Tough
Economy,** Jonni McCoy
The Family Budget Blueprint, Martin Samson
The Family CFO, Marie Claire Allvine
The Magic of Household Budgeting, Kenneth Harmon
The Money Saving Mom's Budget, Crystal Pane
Time To Wake Up: Save Money, Lawrence Burns

FINDING NEW MONEY

1,000 Best eBay Power Seller Secrets, Greg Holden
**555 Ways To Earn Extra Money: The Ultimate Idea
Book For Supplementing Your Income,**
Jay Conrad Levinson
Comforts of Home: Thrifty and Chic Decorating Ideas,
Caroline Clifton-Mogg
eBay For Dummies, Marsha Collier
**Everything You Need To Know About Garage
and Yard Sales,** Jon Fulghum
**Fix It, Clean It, and Make It Last, The Ultimate Guide
To Making Your Household Items Last Forever,**
The Editors of FC&A Publishing
**Flanagan's Smart Home, The 98 Essentials
For Starting Out, Starting Over, Scaling Back,**
Barbara Flanagan
Flea Market Style, Emily Chalmers
Garage Sale America, Bruce Littlefield
Home Renovation Checklist, Robert Irwin

**House Poor, How To Buy and Sell Your Home
Come Bubble or Bust,** June Fletcher
How Moms Are Making Money On eBay, Charity Cason
How To Sell Clothing, Shoes, and Accessories On eBay,
Entrepreneur Press
I Brake For Yard Sales, Lara Spencer
Little Guide To Vintage Shopping, Melody Fortier
Refresh Your Home, Editors of *The Family Handiman*
Save Money: Thrift and Consignment Shopping,
Sandi Lynn
Secondhand Chic, Christa Weil
Stop Throwing Money Away, Jamie Novak
The 7 Essential Steps To Successful eBay Marketing,
Janelle Elms
The Complete Idiot's Guide To eBay, Skip McGrath
The Domestic Diva's Guide To Thrift Store Shopping,
Kathy London
The Homemade Home, Sania Pell
The Official eBay Bible, Jim Griffith
The Rag Street Journal, Elizabeth Mason
The Rummager's Handbook, R.S. McClurg
The Ultimate Consignment Thrift Store Guide,
Carol Schneider
Thrift Score, Al Hoff
Thrifty Chic Interior Style, Liz Bauwens
Tossed and Found, Barbara Tobias

LIVING RICHLY ON A BUDGET

**Give Yourself A Raise: Commonsense Sense Principles
To Help You Think, Act and Live More Abundantly,**
Travis Young
Living Rich By Spending Smart, Gregory Karp
**Money, Money, Money: The Search For Wealth
and The Pursuit of Happiness,** Michael Toms
and Marsha Sinetar

Spend Well, Live Rich, Michelle Singletary
**Stop Acting Rich: And Start Living Like
    A Real Millionaire,** Thomas J. Stanley
**The Five Lessons A Millionaire Taught Me About Life
    and Wealth,** Richard Paul Evans
**The Richest Man in Babylon, The Secrets
    of The Ancients,** George S. Clason
The Ten Commandments of Financial Happiness,
    Jean Chatzky
The Ultimate Cheapskate's Road Map To True Riches,
    Jeff Yeager
Wealth: Money Mastery, Management and Mindset,
    Robert A. Evans
You're So Money: Living Rich, Farnoosh Torabi

MONEY MINDSET

**AdaptAbilty: How To Survive Change You Didn't
    Ask For,** M.J. Ryan
Busting Loose From The Money Game,
    Robert Scheinfeld
Don't Spend Your Raise, Dara Duguay
**Frugillionaire: 500 Fabulous Ways To Live Richly
    and Save A Fortune,** Francine Jay
Going Broke, Stuart Vyse
**Harmonic Wealth: The Secret of Attracting The Life
    You Want,** James Arthur Ray
Let's Get Real About Money, Eric Tyson
Make Money, Not Excuses, Jean Chatzky
On Desire: Why We Want What We Want,
    William B. Irvine
Picking Up The Pennies, Ann S. Danley
**Shameless Shortcuts, 1,027 Tips and Techniques
    That Help You Save Time, Save Money and Save
    Work Every Day!,** Edited by Fern Marshall Bradley
    and the Editors of *Yankee Magazine*

Sound Health, Sound Wealth, Luanne Oakes, Ph.D.
Sudden Money: Managing Windfalls, Susan Bradley
Sway, The Irresistible Pull of Irrational Behavior,
Ori Brafman and Rom Brafman
The Difference, Jean Chatzky
The Four Spiritual Laws of Prosperity, Edwene Gaines
The Frugal Millionaires, Jeff Lehman
The Millionaire Mind, Thomas J. Stanley, Ph.D.
The New Frugality, How To Consume Less, Save More
and Live Better, Chris Farrell
The Psychology of Money, Michael Argyle
The Soul of Money, Lynne Twist
The Truth About Money, Ric Edelman
Why Smart People Do Stupid Things With Money,
Bert Whitehead
Why Smart People Make Big Money Mistakes—and How
To Correct Them, Lessons from the New Science of
Behavior Economics, Gary Belsky and Thomas Gilovich
Why Smart People Make Money Mistakes—and How
To Correct Them, Gary Belsky and Thomas Gilovich

SHOPPING ADDICTION

Addicted To Shopping and Other Issues Women Have
With Money, Karen O'Connor
Born To Spend, Overcoming Compulsive Spending,
Gloria Arenson
Bought Out and Spent! Recovering from Compulsive
Shopping and Spending, Terrence Daryl Shulman
Buyology: Truth and Lies About Why We Buy,
Martin Lindstrom
Decoded: The Science Behind Why We Buy, Phil Barder
I Shop, Therefore I Am: Compulsive Buying
and The Search For Self, April Lane Benson, Ph.D.
In the Red: The Diary of a Recovering Shopaholic,
Alexis Hall

Mind Over Money: Overcoming Money Disorders That Threaten Our Financial Health, Brad Klontz and Ted Klontz

Money Drunk, Money Sober: 90 Day to Financial Freedom, Mark Bryan and Julia Cameron

Not Buying It: My Year Without Shopping, Judith Levine

Overcoming Overspending, A Winning Plan For Spenders and Their Partners, Olivia Mellan with Sherry Christie

Shopism: Why the American Consumer Will Keep Buying No Matter What, Lee Eisenberg

Spent: Memoirs of A Shopping Addict, Avis Cardella

Spent: Sex, Evolution and Consumer Behavior, Geoffrey Miller

The Call of The Mall, Paco Underhill

The Cure For Money Madness, Spencer Sherman

The Money Trap: A Practical Program To Stop Self-Defeating Financial Habits So You Can Reclaim Your Grip On Life, Ron Gallen

To Buy Or Not To Buy: Why We Overshop and How To Stop, April Benson, Ph.D.

Why She Buys: The New Strategy For Reaching The World's Most Powerful Consumers, Bridget Brennan

Why We Buy, The Science of Shopping, Paco Underhill

TEENS AND MONEY MINDSET

Free: Spending Your Time and Money On What Matters Most, Mark Scandrette

High School Money Book, Don Silver

How To Ditch Your Allowance & Be Richer Than Your Parents! Nine Wealth Building Tools To Make A Teen Rich, Patti J. Handy

Money Matters For Teens, Larry Burkett

Money Matters Workbook For Teens, Larry Burkett

Not Your Parents' Money Book, Jean Chatzy
Play The Real-Life Money Game With Your Teen,
Sarah Williamson
Rich Dad, Poor Dad For Teens, Robert Kiyosaki
The Complete Idiot's Guide To Money For Teens,
Susan Shelley
The Teen Girls Gotta Have It Guide To Money,
Jessica Blatt

YOUR RELATIONSHIP WITH MONEY

**Discover The Wealth Within You: A Financial Plan
For Creating a Rich and Fulfilling Life,** Ric Edelman
Financial Fitness Forever, Paul Merriman
and Richard Buck
Make Money, Not Excuses, Jean Chatzky
Master Your Money, Ronald Blue
Money 911, Jean Chatzky
Money and The Pursuit of Happiness,
Richard Trachtman, Ph.D.
Money Mastery, Alan Williams
Money Mastery: Principle-Based Money Management,
Peter Jeppson
Money Therapy, Deborah Price
Money, A Memoir Women, Emotions and Cash,
Liz Perle
Ordinary People, Extraordinary Wealth, Ric Edelman
**Our Money, Ourselves: Redesigning Your Relationship
with Money,** Diane Ealy, Ph.D.
Scroogenomics, Joel Waldfogel
**Start Late, Finish Rich: A No-Fail Plan for Achieving
Financial Freedom At Any Age,** David Bach
The 5 Money Personalities, Scott Palmer
**The Average Family's Guide to Financial Freedom:
How You Can Save a Small Fortune on a
Modest Income,** Bill Toohey and Mary Toohey

The Difference: How Anyone Can Prosper Even In Tough Times, Jean Chatzky

The Emotion Behind Money, Julie Murphy Casserly

The Energy of Money, Maria Nemeth

The Financial Wisdom of Ebenezer Scrooge: Five Principles To Transform Your Relationship With Money, Ted Klontz, Brad Klontz and Rick Kahler

The Get Out of Debt Kit: Your Roadmap To Total Financial Freedom, Deborah McNaughton

The Money Culture, Michael Lewis

The Money Doctor's Guide, Neil Gallagher, Ph.D.

The Money Gym, Nicole Carincross

The Money Therapist: A Woman's Guide, Marcia Brixley

The New Master Your Money Book, Jeremy White

The New Rules of Money: 88 Simple Strategies For Financial Success Today, Ric Edelman

The Six-Day Financial Makeover: Transform Your Financial Life In Less Than A Week!, Robert Pagliarini

The Soul of Money, Transforming Your Relationship With Money and Life, Lynne Twist

The Truth About Money, Ric Edelman

Transforming Your Relationship with Money, Joe Dominguez

Yes You Can... Achieve Financial Independence: A New Diet for Financial Independence, James E. Stowers

You're Broke Because You Want To Be, How To Stop Getting By and Start Getting Ahead, Larry Winget

Your Money or Your Life: Nine Steps To Transforming Your Relationship With Money and Achieving Financial Independence, Vicki Robin

Your Money or Your Life: Transforming Your Relationship With Money, Vicki Robin

Your Money Personality, Kathleen Gurney
Your Money Style, Olivia Mellan

WEDDINGS ON A BUDGET

1,000 Best Wedding Bargains, Insider Secrets From Industry Experts, Sharon Naylor

A Fairy Tale Affair: How To Plan A Fabulous Destination Wedding On A Shoestring Budget, Deborah McKenzie

Bridal Bargains, Denise Fields

Budget Weddings For Dummies, Meg Schneider

DIY Bride: Beautiful Bouquets: Create Your Dream Wedding On A Budget, Khris Cochran

Do It For Less! Weddings: How To Create Your Dream Wedding Without Breaking the Bank, Denise Vivaldo

E-Plan Your Wedding, Crystal Melendez

How To Have A Fabulous Wedding For $10,000 or Less: Creating Your Dream Day With Romance, Grace and Style, Sharon Naylor

How To Have An Elegant Wedding For $5,000 or Less: Achieving Beautiful Simplicity Without Mortgaging Your Future, Jan Wilson and Wilson Hickman

How To Plan and Throw The Picture Perfect Wedding Without Spending Too Much To Glamorize It All, Brently Clemantin

How To Plan Your Own Wedding and Save Thousands without Going Crazy, Tracy Leigh

How To Save Money By Planning Your Own Wedding, Melinda Cooper

How To Save Money On Your Wedding Day, C.B. Foster

One Perfect Day, Rebecca Mead

The Frugal Bride, Cynthia Clumeck Mucanick

Wedding Decor Made Easy, Sandi and Gregg Alcut

Wedding On A Budget: 120 Ways To Cut Wedding Costs, Cara Davis

Wedding On A Budget: Save Your Money, Ora Rosalin
Your Beautiful Wedding On Any Budget, Todd Outcalt
Your Wedding On Any Shoestring, Sandra Lee Schubert

WOMEN AND MONEY MINDSET

Girl, Get Your Money Straight, Glinda Bridgforth
Money Girls' Ten Steps To A Debt-Free Life,
    Laura D. Adams
Nice Girls Don't Get Rich, Lois P. Frankel
On My Own Two Feet: A Modern Girl's Guide
    To Personal Finance, Tanisha Thakor and Sharon Kedar
Prince Charming Isn't Coming, Barbara Stanny
Smart Women Finish Rich, Nine Steps
    To Achieving Financial Security
    and Funding Your Dreams, David Bach
Twenty-Five Day Money Makeover for Women,
    Francine Huff

*(Also see the Suggested Reading Lists in the back
of our two other books on saving.)*

SENIOR SUPPLEMENT
IF YOU ARE A SENIOR, REMEMBER TO ASK FOR YOUR DISCOUNT!

When it comes to discounts, the phrase "If you don't ask, you don't get" really counts. Be a proud senior, as are both Heidi and Sam (55+). Heavens knows there are downsides of aging, but there are also perks for having stuck it out for this long. If you are a senior or love someone who is, remember to ask for the senior discounts everywhere you conduct commerce. Everywhere you ask? Yes, because we will bet that the list below includes at least a handful of establishments that you hadn't thought of asking for a discount until now. Print out the list, commit it to memory, and patronize the places that are generous and smart enough to encourage their senior clientele.

RESTAURANTS:
Apple-bee's: 15% off with Golden Apple Card (60+)
Arby's: 10% off (55+)
Ben & Jerry's: 10% off (60+)
Bennigan's: Discount varies by location (60+)
Bob's Big Boy: Discount varies by location (60+)
Boston Market: 10% off (65+), Burger King: 10% off (60+)
Chick-Fil-A: 10% off or free small drink or coffee (55+)
Chili's: 10% off (55+)
CiCi's Pizza: 10% off (60+)
Denny's: 10% off, 20% off for AARP members (55 +)
Dunkin' Donuts: 10% off or free coffee (55+)
Einstein's Bagels: 10% off baker's dozen of bagels (60+)
Fuddrucker's: 10% off any senior platter (55+)
Gatti's Pizza: 10% off (60+)
Golden Corral: 10% off (60+)
Hardee's: $0.33 beverages everyday (65+)
IHOP: 10% off (55+)

Jack in the Box: Up to 20% off (55+)
KFC: Free small drink with any meal (55+)
Krispy Kreme: 10% off (50+)
Long John Silver's: Various discounts at locations (55+)
McDonald's: Discounts on coffee everyday (55+)
Mrs. Fields: 10% off at participating locations (60+)
Shoney's: 10% off
Sonic: 10% off or free beverage (60+)
Steak 'n Shake: 10% off every Monday & Tuesday (50+)
Subway: 10% off (60+)
Sweet Tomatoes: 10% off (62+)
Taco Bell : 5% off; free beverages for seniors (65+)
TCBY: 10% off (55+)
Tea Room Cafe 10% off (50+)
Village Inn: 10% off (60+)
Waffle House: 10% off every Monday (60+)
Wendy's: 10% off (55+)
Whataburger: 10% off (62+)
White Castle : 10% off (62+)

RETAIL & APPAREL:

Banana Republic 30% off (50+)
Bealls: 20% off first Tuesday of each month (50+)
Belk's: 15% off first Tuesday of every month (55+)
Big Lots: 30% off
Bon-Ton Dept 15 % off on senior discount days (55+)
C.J. Banks: 10% off every Wednesday (50+)
Clarks : 10% off (62+)
Dress Barn: 20% off (55+)
Goodwill: 10% off one day a week
    (date varies by location)
Hallmark: 10% off one day a week
    (date varies by location)
K-Mart: 40% off (Wednesdays only) (50+)
Kohl's: 15% off (60+)

Modell's Sporting Goods: 30% off
Rite Aid: 10% off on Tuesdays & 10% off prescriptions
Ross Stores: 10% off every Tuesday (55+)
The Salvation Army Thrift Stores: Up to 50% off (55+)
Stein Mart: 20% off red dot/clearance items first Monday
   of every month (55+)

GROCERIES:

Albertson's: 10% off first Wednesday of each month (55+)
American Discount Stores: 10% off every Monday (50+)
Compare Foods Supermarket: 10% off every Wednesday (60+)
DeCicco Family Markets: 5% off every Wednesday (60+)
Food Lion: 60% off every Monday (60+)
Fry's Supermarket: Free Fry's VIP Club Membership
   & 10% off every Monday (55+)
Great Valu Food Store: 5% off every Tuesday (60+)
Gristedes Supermarket: 10% off every Tuesday (60+)
Harris Teeter: 5% off every Tuesday (60+)
Hy-Vee: 5% off one day a week (date varies by location)
Kroger: 10% off (date varies by location)
Morton Williams Supermarket: 5% off every Tuesday (60+)
The Plant Shed: 10% off every Tuesday (50+)
Publix: 15% off every Wednesday (55+)
Rogers Marketplace: 5% off every Thursday (60+)
Uncle Guiseppe's Marketplace: 15% off (62+)

TRAVEL :

Airlines: Alaska Airlines: 50% off (65+)
American Airlines: Various discounts for 50% off
   non-peak periods (Tuesdays - Thursdays) (62+) and up
   (call before booking for discount)
Continental Airlines: No initiation fee for Continental
   Presidents Club & special fares for select destinations
Southwest Airlines: Various discounts for ages 65 and up
   (call before booking for discount)

United Airlines: Various discounts for ages 65 and up
(call before booking for discount)
U.S. Airways: Various discounts for ages 65 and up
(call before booking for discount)
Rail: Amtrak: 15% off (62+)
Bus: Greyhound: 15% off (62+) Trailways Transportation
System: various discounts for ages 50+
Car Rental: Alamo Car Rental: Up to 25% off for
AARP members
Avis: Up to 25% off for AARP members
Budget Rental Cars: 40% off; up to 50% off for
AARP members (50+)
Dollar Rent-A-Car: 10% off (50+)
Enterprise Rent-A-Car: 5% off for AARP members
Hertz: Up to 25% off for AARP members
National Rent-A-Car: Up to 30% off for AARP members

OVERNIGHT ACCOMMODATIONS:

Holiday Inn: 20-40% off depending on location (62+)
Best Western: 40% off (55+)
Cambria Suites: 20%-30% off (60+)
Waldorf Astoria - NYC: $5,000 off nightly rate for
Presidential Suite (55+)
Clarion Motels: 20%-30% off (60+)
Comfort Inn: 20%-30% off (60+)
Comfort Suites: 20%-30% off (60+)
Econo Lodge: 40% off (60+)
Hampton Inns & Suites: 40% off when booked 72 hours
in advance
Hyatt Hotels: 25%-50% off (62+)
InterContinental Hotels Group: Various discounts
at all hotels (65+)
Mainstay Suites: 10% off with Mature Traveler's Discount
(50+); 20%-30% off (60+)
Marriott Hotels: 25% off (62+)

Motel 6: Stay Free Sunday nights (60+)
Myrtle Beach Resort: 30% off (55+)
Quality Inn: 40%-50% off (60+)
Rodeway Inn: 20%-30% off (60+)
Sleep Inn: 40% off (60+)

ACTIVITIES & ENTERTAINMENT:

AMC Theaters: Up to 30% off (55+)
Bally Total Fitness: $100 off memberships (62+)
Busch Gardens Tampa, FL: $13 off one-day tickets (50+)
Carmike Cinemas: 35% off (65+)
Cinemark/Century Theaters: Up to 35% off
Massage Envy - NYC: 20% off all "Happy Endings" (62+)
U.S. National Parks: $10 lifetime pass; 50% off additional
    services including camping (62+)
Regal Cinemas: 50% off
Ripley's Believe It Or Not: @ off one-day ticket (55+)
SeaWorld, Orlando, FL : $3 off one-day tickets (50+)

CELL PHONE DISCOUNTS:

AT&T: Special Senior Nation 200 Plan $19.99/month (65+)
Jitterbug: $10/month cell phone service (50+)
Verizon Wireless: Verizon Nationwide 65 Plus Plan
    $29.99/month (65+)

MISCELLANEOUS:

Great Clips: $8 off haircuts (60+)
Supercuts: $8 off haircuts (60+)

Whether or not you look like or feel like you are of "senior" age, go out there and claim the discounts that you qualify for! Remember, YOU must ASK for your discount. "No ask; no discount!" Even if you are not of the "senior" age, you know someone who is.

MORE PRAISE FOR
TheSmartestWay™ to Save
Why You Can't Hang Onto Money and What To Do About It

"There are not only hundreds of tips in this book but it is chock full of websites and other resources that provide additional information and services that one would need on their journey, and they are all right there at your fingertips. You cannot read it all the way through without getting excited about your financial future."

—Jim Davidson,
nationally syndicated columnist

"I'm going to give this book to my 20-year-old daughter. It is easy to comprehend and it will keep her attention because there is a story in each chapter. It will help reinforce some of the lessons I've been trying to teach her as she has grown up."

—Michael L. Remington,
Financial Advisor

"Heidi and Sam, I just wanted to let you know that I am reading your book. It's been a little slow going because I am in denial about my financial responsibility. However, I have every intention of reading it page by page and so far it has been very insightful. I would love to see this as required reading for all young people before they develop bad habits such as mine."

—Debbie Bennett,
Fitness Instructor

"This book is your real-world, step-by-step, easy-to-apply guide to saving money on any budget. It isn't only information, it's motivational. It gives you the confidence and know-how to start taking the necessary steps to stop excess spending and start saving. I would recommend it to anyone looking to gain control of their financial future."

—John Rachlin,
attorney

"These were all ideas we grew up with but haven't been taught to our younger generations. This book should be in every household today and should be referred to often. It is easy to read, but I would not recommend you read the entire book at once, since you need to absorb it. It explains how to avoid the new ways "the money machine" has devised to separate you from your money. Your investment in this book will return to you manifold. Enjoy!"

—Myriam-Rose Kohn,
Certified Personal Branding Strategist

"This book was perfect for my wife and me. We consider ourselves to be fairly financially savvy, but this book offered great tips on saving, discipline, and general money management that we found very helpful. We've implemented several of the strategies and are already seeing results@ Thank you, Heidi and Sam, for such a great resource."

—Adam Bendorf,
musician

"I am going to make certain my two boys read and absorb Sam's 26 Principles of Financial Independence. I myself found the book had many practical ideas that I hope to personally implement."

—Randal Boggin,

Real Estate Executive

"This is a really excellent, practical, and simple guide that contains a great deal of basic wisdom that so many have not learned or have forgotten."

—John O'Connor,
financial advisor

"This book handles all aspects of dealing with money. The authors learned in their childhoods how to make do for food, gifts, and all the necessities of life. I agree it's important in parenting children to set limits on money and role model thrift and spending wisely."

—Jerry Swinnerton, M.A.,
social worker

"I've been a fairly frugal guy and always paid myself first. But after following the advice of financial gurus for decades, I've watch my investments get hammered. That, combined with a new baby at 50, makes saving money and priority spending all the more important. I find this book is truly sage advice. It'll pay for itself in about 12 seconds."

—John Feist,
television and film writer/producer/director

"This book is so deceptively simple and reader-friendly that you almost don't notice until you've finished how comprehensive it is. Replete with wise and immediately practicable suggestions about how to use money to enhance your life, it is peppered with meaningful anecdotes and money stories about the authors and those people who helped them shape their money behavior. These stories foster a bond between the writers and their readers, facilitating change. The book's three parts encourage a reader to focus on money through three different lenses: in relation to oneself, in relation to others, and in relation to the larger world. This variety of perspectives can't help but expand the consciousness of someone who doesn't customarily look at his or her spending and saving habits objectively. In addition, Freshman and Clingen offer up a panoply of tools for managing your money, getting out from under debt, and saving for the future—a richness of resource I've rarely seen in other financial self-help books. Anyone who follows their detailed suggestions for saving money on food, clothing, transportation, travel, and entertainment—and heeds their shrewd advice on protecting oneself from scams and other fraud—should be able to go forth unafraid, ready, willing, and able to move toward financial independence."

—April Lane Benson, Ph.D.,
*author of "To Buy or Not to Buy: Why We
Overshop and How to Stop"*

"Written in a language that we can all understand, this book shows all members of the family how they can work together in order to deal with difficult times. The authors have taken their own personal experiences and expertise and combined them to the reader's benefit. You might not be able to use all of the tips, but you will find a handful that fit your own situation. Definitely a book you want to keep some where handy."

—Cyrus Webb,
talk show host

"What a relief to have found this book for my wife and I to read. Now we are agreeing on the direction on how to save, spend, and invest our money. This book would be an excellent text book for schools to teach students the basic principles of money and how to save and spend responsibly. We are definitely saving this book for our 8- and 10-year old children to read! Thank you."

—Bruce Nyznik,
film editor

"Since we are just entering retirement, this book comes at exactly the right time. Not only does it re-affirm our lifelong spending and saving practices, it offers valuable suggestions and new ways on conserving and extending our financial resources for the unknown future. We don't have time to earn it again. For us, this book will be our guide to resource management."

—Ray Detournay

"Over our married life, I've been the keeper of the household books while my husband was in charge of the "big picture." In retirement, it is necessary to meld those elements. This book has proved invaluable as a guide for developing a plan for asset/expense management and control A side benefit is that my husband now appreciates how well I've managed our expenses all these years."

—Louise Detournay

"It's not what you earn, it's what you keep. Instead of playing financial offense killing ourselves for large incomes, we should be playing good financial defense, buying only what we truly need. This book turns over all stones in how to save smart. This book does a great job of explaining Sam's principles in detail so you can follow them."

—Steve Burns,
Amazon Top 500 Reviewer

"This book has helped me with suggestions on how to live better on a limited income, and it has inspired me to start saving again, "for a rainy day.""

—Emily Lanier

"The authors offer solid plans to help make correct financial choices. They boil down the concepts and eliminate the excuses. You may find some of the concepts old fashioned, but it doesn't mean that we shouldn't try them in these trying times."

—Charles Evans,
Amazon Top 100 Reviewer

"This book is particularly important during what appears to be a recession that could become a depression. The authors have done a great job of explaining what may have been obvious to those who lived through the Great Depression, but most Americans have no idea of how to live in strained times. This book will be essential to them."

—Ronald E. Stackler

This book needs to be in the hands of every high school student. The tools taught in this book will set the foundation for financial success that every parent wants for their kids... and themselves! This book is easy to read, yet filled with invaluable information for every age group. As a money coach for teens, I completely respect and support the material taught in this book."

—Patti Handy,
author of "How to Ditch Your Allowance and Be Richer Than Your Parents: 9 Wealth-Building Tools to Make a Teen Rich"

INDEX

INDEX